ARTISTS OF MAUI

ARTISTS

OF MAUI

A COLLECTION OF ARTWORK WITH TEXT AND DESIGN BY RICHARD P. WIRTZ

ARTISTS OF MAUI

Text and Design by
Richard P. Wirtz
Skipper Printing and Graphics Art Director

Photo Consultant and
Cover and Contents page photos
Russell F. Beach
Avco Everett Research Laboratory, Inc.
Photographic Engineer

Published by
SUMAC Publishing Company
P. O. Box 1646
Makawao, HI 96768
Peter and Susan McCormick, *owners*

The publisher has made every effort to credit sources properly. If there are any questions concerning this, please contact the publisher and corrections will be made in future editions.

Prepared by
Skipper Printing and Graphics, Inc.
Wailuku, Hawaii
Richard Wirtz, *Art Director*
Ted Larimer, *Consulting Editor and Typographer*
Eric Rognstad, *Layout*
Sue Wirtz, *Research and Layout*
Ron Reuter, *Technical Consultant*
James Thompson, *Camera*

The text for this book is set in 11 point Candida with heads in Candida Bold and Grayda Bold Script on an Itek 2110 photocompositor. Color separations and printing in Singapore by Tien Wah Press (PTE.) Inc. on 150gsm Royal Sword Matt Artpaper with 140gsm KNP Text paper end sheets and Duralin over 2.5mm board cover with 115gsm Royal Sword Artpaper jacket. Coordination with Singapore and quality control by Heritage Graphics Inc., Richard W. Lyday, president.

Library of Congress Catalog Card No. 85-61706
ISBN: 0-918345-02-2

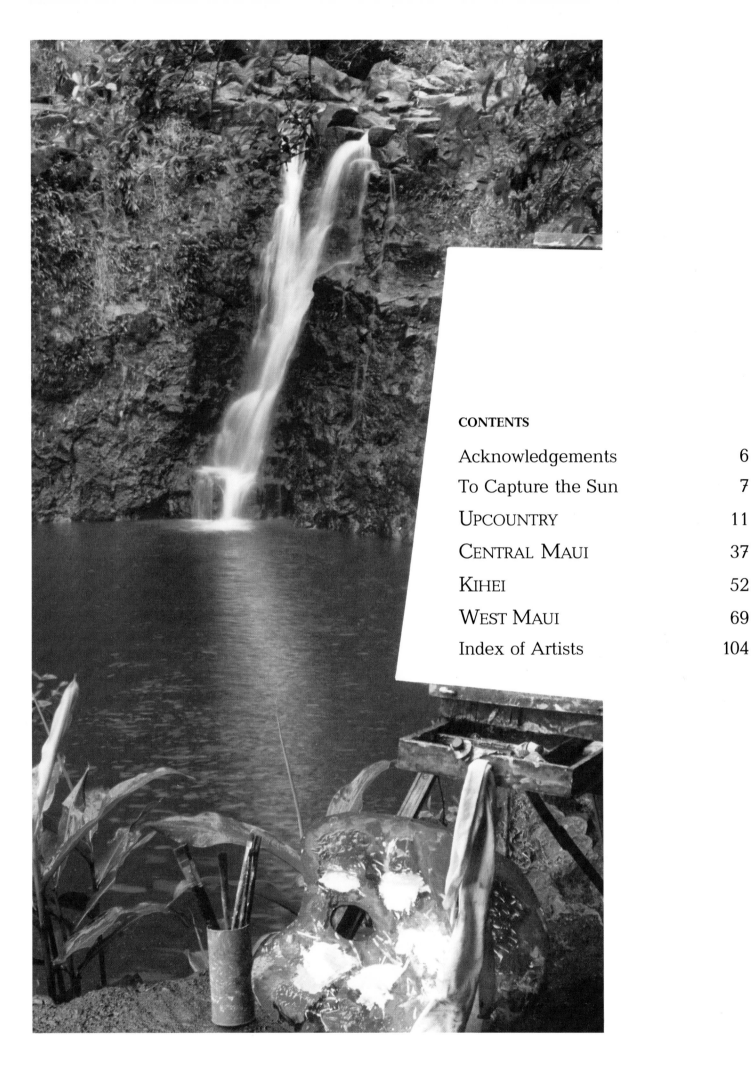

CONTENTS

DEDICATION

The publisher dedicates this compilation of
art to Florida Evans and the memory of
Sanford G. Evans.

ACKNOWLEDGEMENTS

This project has been made possible by the
help of many people beginning with the
artists themselves and include: Pierre of
Lahaina Studios, John Motelewski and Steve
Wilson, photographers; The Maui Historical
Society, Muffie Mitchell director; Paul
McCormick, Julie Bearman, Sanford and
Nelda Evans, Jr., Sarfaraz and Joy Siddiqi,
Richard and Sara Rolfe, Morse and Caroline
Craig, Dick Lyday, Virginia Wirtz, Merlyn
Hodge, Jerry Skipper; The Hawaii State
Library, Kahului and Makawao Branches and
the library at Maui Community College.

We also thank Bob Krauss and *The
Honolulu Advertiser* for the use of his May
11, 1962 "In One Ear" laundromat story, and
Brian Nicol, *Honolulu* and *Aloha* magazines
for valuable research material.

TO CAPTURE THE SUN

WHEN MAUI, the heroic demigod of Polynesian legend, climbed the slopes of Haleakala, he blazed a trail that creative souls have aspired to ever since. And when, with his fishnet, he snared the rising sun and slowed its travels for his mother's sake, he unwittingly created a haven for artists; for the day still travels more slowly on Maui than anywhere else I know.

Talking to the thirty or so artists whose life and work is displayed on the following pages, certain themes echoed softly through our conversations like the constant refrain of surf. Maui's special sense of space and time was mirrored in words like, "relaxes," "friendly," "informal," or in comments like Guy Buffet's: "...it's the smiling cows of Makawao, and sunset drinks at Kimo's. It's Hasegawa General Store, George Pahoa and Tiny's Hana tour bus. It's Carl Lindquist and The Sons of Hawaii. It's secret valleys, the waterfalls and misty hues. It's 'da best,'..."

Rippling beneath comments such as these is always the massive framework of space created by Maui's two mountain ranges. Any sculptor worth his salt knows that as he builds form he defines space, architects do the same. Maui's mountains enlarge the sky and diminish the size of man—a notion that Aldo Leopold would certainly approve. The resulting relationship releases man's spirit to soar, or so I believe. It then becomes possible to accomplish a supreme act of imagination—to ascend the great humpback slope of Haleakala with only a fishnet, or paints, a brush and canvas, and capture the world's source of warmth. And it matters little if the artist's mountain is a roadside hibiscus or shadows on the forest floor.

"I rediscovered nature coming to Maui" is a comment I frequently heard and bears out the central fact of life on Maui—nature. It's not unlike the lessons learned in school about China. How this country was so large it couldn't be conquered, but rather always absorbed and transformed its enemies and remained China. Nature on Maui has some of that largeness—although it is more vulnerable and shrinking. Yet nature's color, drama and life rhythms are still dominant enough here to possess most of the inhabitants. It is difficult not to turn outward on Maui, especially for artists, which may or may not account for the general absence of what we call "modern art" or purely abstract work.

The marketplace also exerts a selective force. Visitors from around the globe make up the largest segment of support for the art community. And they seldom travel or vacation here looking for "downtown New York" artwork. It can be argued that the marketplace, visitors, local institutions and patrons are a product of what this island essentially is. Thus the selection of artists represented in this book reflects more of a selective and transforming process that Maui makes rather than the opinion of any individual.

For all this, Maui, situated as it is in the late twentieth century in the middle of the Pacific, provides the artist with a remarkable measure of freedom. Communication and travel being what they are, there isn't an artist working here who is unaware of Shang Dynasty bronzes, the acropolis or William deKooning's "Marilyn Monroe." That most of the artwork appears to be informed by the work of the Impressionists and Expressionists speaks again to the nature of light and color here on Maui. But hints of every form and style known can be found here. There are artists who mix and merge cultures and style with reckless abandon.

Is there a "Maui" art form or style that is distinct from other styles being generated in other places around the globe? I don't believe so. The work done here can not even be considered eclectic. Distinctly diverse would be a better characterization of the work as a whole. For Maui is a gentle and accepting place, allowing each artist to pursue his or her search for beauty, truth and skill along whatever path moves them.

There is also a great wealth of new talent on the island which may account for much of the diversity we see. Less than a third of the artists represented grew up in the islands—survived its school systems, changes of lifestyle, explosion of growth, and have a childhood with Hawaii in common. Should the influx of artists from other parts of the world stabilize, it may come to pass in the years ahead that a distinctive Maui style or form will emerge.

Meanwhile each artist answers the drummer of his choice and scales the mountain of his choice. And although we could not include all their work or the work of every artist on the island, we celebrate them all with the work we have been able to display. I am thankful to all of them for being who they are, and for their considerable help and patience with this project.

HUBBELL: *Lahaina Days, 4' x 8', ceramic mural*

ROMAN HUBBELL:

Earth, Water, Air and Fire

*T*he boiler room of the old Pauwela cannery was just an open shed affair attached to the main building before Roman Hubbell rented it. With castoff materials from the old King Theatre and Paia Mercantile, he built a multilevel studio to house his kiln, wheels, clay storage, work and office space. It is here that Roman brings together the four magic elements of the ancients—earth, water, air and fire—to create a wide diversity of images and art products: ceramic tile murals, large sculptural pots and wood sculpture.

Roman originated from the Grand Canyon area and grew up and studied in California. While still a teenager, Roman acquired a formal grounding in the art of pottery from Jean Campbell. And as he worked and developed, the art of Japanese potter Hamada and American painter Jackson Pollock shaped the direction he was to take. Roman first arrived in Hawaii in 1969 to teach pottery making at Oahu's North Shore Environmental Center.

In 1971 Roman was invited to Scotland to instruct at the original Findhorn Foundation. Returning a year later, Roman taught and worked at the West Los Angeles Potters Studio before opening a private studio in Malibu in 1974. His works of this period, primarily custom interior design pieces, are found today in the elegant homes and private collections of some of the West Coast's most prominent art patrons.

Late in 1978, Roman abandoned the frenzy of the California scene to establish a permanent studio on Maui. "Maui graces us," Roman said, and he attempts to the return the blessing with his craft.

Hubbell is a foremost exponent of the intricate and time-consuming glazing techniques perfected during the T'ang and Ming Dynasties. Each piece receives three or more separate glazes, controlled applications of color. This multiple glazing instills a tri-dimensional effect to the pottery's surface, adding a dynamic sense of aliveness to Roman's work. He waves aside cultural boundaries, using form, technique and motifs from a wide range of time and space to create pieces that are truly classic and enduring.

Metamorphosis, 18"x12", Albany Slip Routile Glaze

UPCOUNTRY

THE ARTISTS represented in this first section, beginning with Roman Hubbell, live and work on the slopes of Haleakala in a broad, vaguely defined area known as "Upcountry." It rises vertically from 1,000 feet to 4,000 feet above sea level, and wraps around the mountain from Makawao on the north to Kula and Ulupalakua on the south. Farming and ranching have characterized this area for more than a century. With beef products went potatoes, onions and coffee, grown to help feed miners during the California gold rush. Chinese farmers moved in during the 1880s and '90s, having gained their freedom from plantation crews. The narcissus you spot growing wild in the pastures is a mark of their presence.

The Japanese followed, and with them came Genichi Kajiya with persimmon slips he had bought from a man who carried them from Japan. By the mid 1930s, Kajiya and his wife had turned 7½ acres into a flourishing persimmon grove. The area also supports fields of blue-green foliage that yield the colorful carnations that lei makers seek, as well as towering windbreak eucalyptus, plum and peach trees, chrysanthemums, camellias, delphiniums, and the recently introduced rainbow-hued proteas. The greenhouses, flower and vegetable farms are framed on the mauka or upland elevations by rolling pastures and forest groves, and at the lower elevations by broad sweeps of waving cane and regimented rows of pineapple.

The rose is Maui's official flower and this came about as a result of the enterprise of James Makee, a Scotish sea captain. At Ulupalakua, the southern end of Upcountry, Makee established a thriving independent community with a decidedly aristocratic flavor—Rose Ranch. A steam mill processed as much as 1,800,000 pounds of sugar a year, and ranch hands cured and packed beef for the whalers and tanned hides for the California trade. Makee's nursery and gardens were grand and "pink cottage roses grew everywhere." Eighty torchbearers were turned out to escort King Kalakaua and Queen Kapiolani to the specially built white frame house (now gone) on the occasion of their "royal progress" through the islands. Rose Ranch was a focal point for the era that knew bowling on the lawn, croquet, conversation at an elegantly appointed table and waltzing with visiting naval officers. There are descriptions of the six Makee girls racing their horses across the landscape with their colorful pa'u skirts streaming behind like great wings. And it is said that the old captain's ghost still walks among the 15,000 evergreen and eucalyptus trees he planted.

Ulupalakua at one end of upcountry and Makawao at the other host the summer season of rodeos and polo matches that highlight ranching activity today. In the early 1900s Ikua Purdy of Ulupalakua broke the steer roping record while winning a world championship in Cheyenne, Wyoming. Today the big event is the Makawao Rodeo, a Fourth of July weekend extravaganza that sports a full parade and draws wranglers from all the islands. The arena that makes this all possible in Makawao was begun in 1955 with the support of two members of one of Maui's most outstanding polo teams, Richard "Manduke" Baldwin and Harold "Oskie" Rice.

The often rainbow-arched Makawao, gateway to upcountry, has seen the greatest vacillation in growth over the years. When the Fourth Marine Division established a camp at "Giggle Hill" in nearby Kokomo during World War II, businesses by the dozens sprouted up to service the marines. The end of the war left Makawao a ghost town hangout for carousers. Recent opening of subdivisions that have turned acres of pastureland into pavement have been accompanied by new stores, selling designer boots and French wine in windows that once displayed gallon jars filled with three-for-a-penny jawbreakers and licorice sticks as well as homegrown produce. Makawao grows again, its community association committed to preserving a town where folks ride to work on horseback.

But not all Makawao is cowboys and polo ponies. In a gracious Mediterranean-style mansion built by Harry and Ethel Baldwin in 1917 resides the Hui Noeau, "Club of Skills." They are a non-profit organization fostering arts and crafts at this upcountry estate since 1976. The stables at "Kaluanui" have become a ceramics studio, the pantry a darkroom, and the upstairs bedrooms the location of painting, weaving and drawing classes. They also sponsor silkscreening, woodcarving, batik dyeing, lauhala weaving, Hawaiian quilting and haku lei making, as well as putting on several shows each year.

CURTIS WILSON COST:

Studies in Island Tranquility

TO CAPTURE THE SPIRIT OF KULA AND THE REST
OF MAUI IN A WAY THAT IS DISTINCTLY MY OWN

Mango Ladder, ©1981 Curtis Wilson Cost, 18″x 30″, Mixed Media, Private Collection

𝒯here was never a question in his mind of doing anything else. Curtis Wilson Cost can't remember a time when he wasn't drawing in notebooks or doing pen and ink sketches of friends and local scenes. Since his father was an artist, he became an artist.

Curtis grew up in California with paints in the kitchen cabinet, brushes in the sink and canvases stacked against the walls. His dad, James Peter Cost, did nothing but paint, specializing in ocean scenes and later landscapes.

Cost came to Hawaii in 1968, attended Kalani High School where he graduated in 1971. The next year he met Jill, who was to become his wife; and together they traveled back to Carmel where Curtis spent eight months studying art technique with his father.

"By then I had made up my mind to get serious about my painting, to become a professional in the real sense of the word. My father's experience, his teaching and advice gave me the edge I needed."

Returning to Hawaii, Curtis and Jill settled on the lower slopes of Haleakala, Kula—or to some "Cost Country"—a place of weathered clapboard houses, rusting tin roofs, green trees, cattle grazing and rolling meadows.

"My primary aim is to capture the spirit of Kula and the rest of Maui in a way that is distinctly my own. Maui has a sense of peace and a sense of life that can't be compared to anywhere else in the islands."

Ron Ronck of the *Honolulu Advertiser* wrote, "His heightened realistic paintings, with such titles as *Rain in the Valley, Tributary, Horizon Light* and *A Break in the Weather* are studies in island tranquility."

Curtis says, "There's the wonder of Haleakala, the isolation of Hana and lushness of Iao Valley. I've thought of going over to the Big Island to paint...but I never

Jacaranda Season, ©*1983 Curtis Wilson Cost,*
24″ x 48″, Acrylic, Private Collection

Private Landing, ©*1985 Curtis Wilson Cost, 18″ x 24″, Gouache, Private Collection*

© CURTIS WILSON COST

seem to run out of subjects here. In fact, I could probably just sit on our front porch in Kula and paint for weeks."

He started in Kula working in watercolor and has moved through the use of gouache to oils and acrylics. For a while he used just acrylics but has returned lately to oils for larger work and gouache for smaller pieces. "Each medium has possibilities and limitations different from the others. I find it hard to beat oils for the detail work on large canvases."

Cost paints slowly, perhaps spending three months or more on a large painting. One canvas sat on his easel for a year and a half before he felt able to release it. "I lose a certain objectivity working too fast. I'd rather let the work settle into my subconscious. When I feel totally right about it, then it goes out."

About a third of his paintings are commissioned. He sells the rest of his work through his father's gallery in Carmel-By-The-Sea and his studio in Kula. Curtis likes to encourage interested customers to visit his studio, which can be arranged by appointment.

TODD CAMPBELL:

Woodworker, Picture Framer

MASSIVE, SIMPLE SHAPES THAT REVEAL THE
BEAUTIFUL AND INTRICATE DESIGNS OF NATURE

Behind a small gray cottage in Makawao, Todd Campbell lifts a 200- to 250-pound cross-section of Norfolk pine to his band saw. With the same need a potter has to center the mass he works with, Todd will cut off the excess and leave a rough shape that is as balanced as possible. This shape is then turned on a lathe to a rough of the final bowl or platter and allowed to cure for three months. Some woods, especially the more blond ones, Todd will leave outside to allow "spalting," a weathering process which darkens and streaks the wood accenting the grain and providing a nice color variation.

Todd Campbell—of Hawaiian, Chinese and Scottish ancestry—grew up in the Makiki area of Honolulu and moved to Maui in 1978. His wood turning is a self-taught art, and the resulting massive and simple shapes have found their way into private collections across the nation and have been exhibited throughout the state, winning many awards, including two purchases by the Hawaii State Foundation For Culture And The Arts.

Todd works with at least 25 different types of wood gathered throughout the island and brought back to his studio for curing. "Maui is good for this type of work because of the space and the supply of wood. People who know my work will let me know when a tree is being cut, or when they would like one to be removed.

"The bowls shown in the book are Norfolk pine. Each piece is carefully cut so the knots are symmetrical in design. Some shapes I'll use so the knots are toward the bottom where the bowl curves back in making a star-like effect, others just ring the outside. I want each piece to reveal the beautiful and intricate design of nature."

Todd hand rubs the finish on all his bowls. "When I rub, the wood heats up and the finish sinks into the wood. I can control the results better with hand rubbing." A special combination of materials that Todd has discovered gives a deep luster to his pieces.

Walking through Todd's studio and the numerous dated bowl blanks that await final turning, one comes to an adjacent small building. Here Todd has a complete custom framing shop. The combination of both careers allows Todd to be sensitive to the aesthetic values of each. "I enjoy the variation and challenges required in both areas."

RICHARD GALLAGHER:

The Frozen Moment

I WANT MY WORK TO INVOLVE THE VIEWER
JUST AS HAIKU POETRY INVOLVES THE READER

The five years I spent in the Peace Corps really affected my life, my outlook on things," says Richard Gallagher. Originally from Lorain, Ohio, Richard graduated from the University of Detroit with a bachelor's degree in architecture. He had already been working in an architect's office under a work-study program and after getting his degree, Richard continued for about three months before joining the Peace Corps. Two and a half years later when he returned from Somalia, East Africa, Richard found it extremely difficult to get back to work in an office. "I was suffering a kind of reverse culture shock. I seemed to be building paper piles instead of houses. The Peace Corps drew me into construction itself, into the outdoors, into designing and building as a continuous event. And I got to work out my own ideas. So I finally went back and did a second hitch."

Between, around and since these experiences, Richard traveled to the Virgin Islands, Mexico and Europe. "I was always sketching, even back in school and throughout both Peace Corps experiences." During Richard's year and a half in Peru, he met an island boy who invited him to Maui. "I've been on Maui now for twelve years, and it feels like I've been here all my life. Maui provides a base, a home for my art projects and such things as a piano. Drawing tables, easels, and piano are hard things to backpack." The walls of Richard's comfortable and non-ostentatious home are hung with the works of a great variety of artists. His own work appears here and there showing an equally wide range of themes.

"Until recently most of my subjects have been old buildings done in pen and ink with watercolor washes—the architecture interest showing. But I'm moving in new directions now, exploring new media." Richard has developed a keen interest in the Haiku form of poetry and is exploring the inclusion of Haiku in the visual piece. "With Haiku so much is left to the imagination of the reader, and what the reader brings to the piece. So I've experimented with not so crisp forms, and charcoal and pastels, doing landscapes and seascapes."

Richard still works with pen and ink and watercolor washes, but other media as well. His watercolor scapes will include a figure or an unusual natural feature in an almost symbolic manner. The pictures that I saw were highly suggestive and loaded with story innuendo, like frozen moments in an important series of events.

Right: *In Makawao, 14"x 18", Pen, Ink and Watercolor.*
Below: *Ironwood Tree (Olowalu), 19"x 15", Pen, Ink and Watercolor.*

Gallagher

PAMELA HAYES:

A Hibiscus Quest

THE HOMEY PAINTINGS...IN THEIR CONTENTMENT PROVIDE AN ANTIDOTE TO THE MADNESS OF OUR TIMES

amela Hayes moved to Maui seven years ago with a backpack and a box of art supplies. This move fulfilled a long held dream of living someplace beautiful and out of the mainstream of life. However, as all roses have thorns, Pamela discovered that working as a cook in the restaurants of Maui did not provide enough to support a studio and the large oils she had grown accustomed to painting in Los Angeles. Economics forced her into watercolors, and Pam started by painting a common hibiscus in a waterglass. She has been painting with watercolors ever since, frequently returning to paint the common hibiscus. As she puts it, "If the Japanese can paint nothing but bamboo for 10 years, I can do the same for the common hibiscus."

Pam grew up in the San Fernando Valley in Los Angeles, and received her B.A. *magna cum laude* from California State University at Northridge. The last year of college was spent in the "Studies Abroad" program in Florence, Italy. From there she went on to a year of graduate study at the Royal College of Art in London. "These two years in Europe were real growing-up years for me. My attitude toward life and art shifted from the dilettante to the committed artist."

Untitled, 18"x 22",
Watercolor

Sly, 22"x 29",
Watercolor

For the last seven years Pamela has lived in the cool and often wet uplands of Maui, painting steadily and supporting herself as a cook. "Here is the peace and beauty I have always longed for.

"Watercolors are considered by many to be the most difficult medium in painting; once the color is down on paper, nothing can be changed. On the other hand, it is wonderfully spontaneous and the colors can't be surpassed." Pam's paintings play opposite colors against each other to achieve "...the startling beauty of the tropics." Hot pink, orange and red flowers played against the intense blue and greens of foliage, ocean, or sky.

"A good painting should pull the eyes; the colors, lines, subject matter and subtle relationships should cast a spell. Paintings of Mother Nature, flowers and gardens, the homey paintings of a cat curled asleep in its contentment, provide an antidote to the madness of our times." Her watercolors can be found at the Village Gallery in Lahaina or the Makai Gallery in Kihei.

Spring Roses, Oil on Canvas with Koa frame and back,
Free-standing Screen; Woodwork by Paul Kasprzycki

JAN KASPRZYCKI:

Colorist in Love with Paint

MAUI PROVIDES THE QUALITY OF LIGHT.
AND EASE OF LIFESTYLE NEEDED.

Jan Kasprzycki (pronounced Yahn Kas-pris-ski) has successfully achieved in his work a strong balance between realism and abstraction. "I am a colorist," he explains. "I am in love with paint. When I begin painting, I think in abstract terms of form, shape and color...not subject. The realism of the subject is less important to me and more an element of the painting's design. I do love certain subjects [waterlilies, iris, ti leaves are recurring images in Jan's work] but my initial intent is always to create an emotional impact by manipulating color and light."

Impact is also created by the size of Jan's work: large. He enjoys working large which has led to the mural-size screens illustrated here. A rich impasto technique enables him to be more expressive. "Part of the excitement of my work is the application of the brush to canvas. Each stroke is an emotional act, an extension of myself. Changing the attitude with which paint is applied changes the whole piece." Jan will paint the same subject again and again, each time creating a new painting. "Since the subject is less important to me than the light, color and emotion, each time I attempt again

a subject I have done before, I make a new discovery about it."

Jan Kasprzycki was born in Rhode Island and grew up in Southern California. He graduated from Los Angeles Art Center, College of Design, and then helped create the successful graphic design firm of Berryhill/Kasprzycki. Ten years were spent creating advertising, packaging, and annual reports for such major corporate accounts as Max Factor, Hunt/Wesson, 20th Century Fox, Capitol Records and McDonell Douglas.

"It was interesting work, but the need to solve everyone else's creative problems became a chore." Although he did fine art projects for sale and exhibition in his free time, the need to devote more and more time to fine art, and the frustration of not being able to, grew over the years. In 1976 Jan dissolved the design business and moved to Hawaii where "the quality of light and the ease in lifestyle provided the environment needed to create."

Inspired by the dramatic landscapes and abundance of floral growth in the islands, Jan manages to paint nearly everyday. The rest of his time is spent traveling abroad for various business commitments and windsurfing for relaxation.

Yellow Shower Tree, 54"x 98", Oil

RANDY JOSEPH:

Subtle, Flowing Lines

TO SEEK A BALANCE BETWEEN MARINE LIFE
AND ALL THE OTHER LIFE ON THIS PLANET

*T*he son of a commercial fisherman, Randy Joseph grew up on the waters around the Florida Keys. "Wildlife, fish and sea birds, always intrigued me. I came out to Hawaii in 1969, to Maunaolu when there was a junior college there, to study marine science." Randy is currently translating his love and concern for the creatures of the sea into eloquent statements in wood. "There is an increased awareness of the delicate balance between marine life and all the other life forms on this planet. And I like to think that my work participates in that awareness."

While in school on Maui, Randy started doing some landscaping and landscape designing. This provided enough income to begin a sculpture apprenticeship. Following the time-honored Renaissance method of learning, Randy apprenticed with sculptors both here and on the mainland. "I sought out a sculptor in Florida I knew about whose specialty was preditory birds, and studied with him for awhile.

"Henry Moore's recent work has influenced me. Not the big monuments for which he is famous, but rather some recent work I saw while on the east coast this last summer....very simple forms with subtle,

flowing lines. Nature is full of these lines." Randy finds the relationships of natural creatures to each other and to their environment his chief concern. "Maui is one of the best places for feeling that you're part of nature. Nature has always been a big thing with me, perhaps because I'm a Pisces or because I grew up with it.

"The challenge, I think, is to express the beauty of nature's creatures through the natural beauty of wood. It's exciting to discover parallel rhythms or forms echoing forms." Randy works in all available wood types and gets excited about the possibilities developing in the use of local exotic woods such as mango or milo. "I love the natural grain and coloration of wood...to bring out the forms and movement in the wood.

"It used to be a sculptor was restricted to wall hanging reliefs or exterior garden or architectural sculpture. But people are bringing more sculpture into the home. Table sculpture is popular." This turn of popular taste has helped the young sculptor immensely as Randy Joseph has gone from selling under the Banyan tree to signing a gallery contract. "Sixteen pieces sold in the last eight months...it begins to make it all worthwhile."

RICHARD L. NELSON:

The Nature of Nature

I SEEK A MASTERY OF MY CRAFT, A CONTROLLED REFINEMENT BUT
ONLY AS A MEANS THROUGH WHICH THE IDEA CAN BE REVEALED

D ick Nelson is a working artist living high on the slopes of Haleakala—a hermit on the hill perfecting his craft. Yet not entirely isolated as he gives large chunks of his time to conducting seminars and watercolor classes across the West Coast and Hawaii. He enjoys teaching, a natural carry-over from earlier days as chairman of the Punahou art department. Talking with Dick, one is apt to learn as much about the successes and frustrations of his students as about his own work.

But of his own work Dick says, "Hawaii has been my home since I was five years old. The influences of the land, its people and culture have undoubtedly shaped my aesthetic values and perceptions, both intuitively and consciously. Although my professional training on the mainland provided the tools, techniques and aesthetic options, Hawaii generated the ideas."

That mainland education included bachelor's and master's degrees in art education, respectively, from California College of Arts and Crafts and Ohio State University, plus a year's special study program at Yale University. A Marine Corps officer for 23 years, Dick retired from the reserves as a Lieutenant Colonel in 1975, the same year he took leave of the chairmanship of the Punahou art department and became director of the Wailea Arts Center on Maui.

"My earlier interest in painting the particulars of an island scene has given way to more personal interpretations. The visual qualities of land, sea and sky, have replaced descriptions of specific locations. The transparent, translucent and reflecting surfaces of water, responding in fluid rhythm to stable, solid and opaque land forms, provide some of the inspiration for my visual ideas."

The technique behind his work has led Dick into developing a special approach to

Opposite page: Hawaii Bound (San Francisco at the Golden Gate), 22"x 30", Watercolor, Alexander and Baldwin, Inc., Collection

Metamorphosis, 22"x 30", State Foundation For Culture And The Arts

handling color. Through the old notion of using just the primaries to create the whole range of possible hues, Nelson has been able to create some marvelous atmospheric effects while retaining brilliance of color. He is currently marketing his ideas, "Tri-hue," and resultant aids, through his many workshops and seminars.

When asked what living and working on Maui meant to him as an artist, Dick handed me a large binder of slides—watercolors done over the last five or so years. Most of the images were uniquely Maui—waterfalls, clouds, seacoast and the central valley. But what seemed most Maui to me was not the recognizable images but rather the way they had been handled. Maui has always had for me a quiet power, a huge softness, and these qualities could be perceived in the slides.

"If Hawaii is in my painting, it is there more in attitude than subject matter. An attitude nurtured in an environment of gentleness of people and place."

DAVID WARREN:

Art is the Touchstone

THE GRACIOUS DIGNITY OF THE PEOPLE AND THE INCOMPARABLE BEAUTY OF THE ISLANDS

The sky-lit glow that permeates David Warren's studio in Haiku reveals an environment that is comfortable, well-built and, like the adjacent house and grounds, is old enough to have roots of its own. In many ways David's immediate surroundings partake of the gracious dignity he finds so abundant in the islands. He fits easily into this tropical scene, having come a long way from his Minnesota upbringing.

Yet David has never strayed far from his first love; rather he has nursed a lifelong passion for the study of art, history, ideas and current directions which began with instructions as a child at the Walker Art Center in Minneapolis. He continued his art education at the Minneapolis College of Art and Design and the San Francisco Art Institute, where he studied with Richard

Deibenkorn and Nathan Oliviera.

After receiving a B.F.A. in 1963, David spent a number of years traveling around the United States and working in the mainstream of modern art movements. "I was really caught up in the leading edge of events.... The move to Maui altered my view of things and profoundly affected the direction of my art. For one thing, I found myself at peace with my surroundings." David built a home and studio on the slopes of Haleakala and began the rediscovery of nature.

"On Maui I began painting landscapes and figure studies. The gracious dignity of the people and the incomparable beauty of the islands impressed me very early. I studied the cultural history, even took a trip to Kaho'olawe. The experiences, processed through my art, have lead me inward to deal directly with the subjective content and

Above: *Ano Hula, Aquatint on
Six Plates, Private Collection*
Right: *Hula Polu, 24″x 32″, Monotype,
Private Collection*

Hula Lili'i, 24" x 32", Monotype, Private Collection

Kaha'apo-Line Embrace, 36"x 72", Oil, Three Panels, Private Collection

emotion. The surface beauty has become for me a window through which to explore the richness of the human spirit."

David has worked with a wide range of media and treatments of subject matter. At present he is expressing himself in three forms: oil on canvas, etching and monotype— an original oil, painted on a plate, transferred to rag paper, then reworked with watercolor and oil stick. "The flexibility and potential of the monotype process are so great that I am constantly challenged to harness the explosion of color and form to create a focused image."

David's treatment of subjects is moving beyond realism or naturalism. Some of his early concerns for the pure elements of design are beginning to re-emerge in his latest efforts to create aesthetic equivalents of the human spirit. "I will keep growing, exploring. Art is the touchstone of my life."

Hawaii, 15"x 18", Private Collection

PAMELA ANDELIN:

The Act of Painting

I LIKE TO EXPERIMENT IN DIFFERENT MEDIA, AND
MOST OF ALL I LIKE TO WORK OUTDOORS ON LOCATION

*A*ll of my dad's family are artists, painters and gallery owners," said Pamela Andelin. "They all tried to warn me off art as a career..." However, art for Pamela has always been a part and extension of who she is. A painting career, as inevitable as a sunrise, was only a matter of time. "I love painting, the act of painting. I come away from it refreshed."

Pamela was born in Honolulu before the attack on Pearl Harbor and grew up in Kaimuki "...next door to Hilo Hattie." She was educated in California, mixing business courses in with the art major and eventually found herself back in Hawaii, on Lanai. "Dad kept working in Hollywood and I got back to Hawaii as fast as I could." It was to Lanai that Emerson Andelin, Pamela's father, eventually retired, giving up his many art clubs and joining his daughter to teach what he knew and continue his painting. "My dad was really dedicated: an artist's artist. When he wasn't painting, he was reading about painters."

Pamela returned to Honolulu where she did a variety of things to make a living: stewardess, dental assistant, beach girl for the Halekulani. "It was a wild and busy period." As events stabilized for Pamela, she ran into Pil Soon Conklin. "She thought I had talent and encouraged me by waving checks in front of my eyes. She had cancer at the time and I was able to help her by going out with her, painting on new locations. I learned a lot from her. We gave to each other, it was a neat experience and a real turning point for me."

Pamela began taking courses at the Academy of Arts and at the University of Hawaii from Lloyd Sexton. She displayed and sold work from the zoo fence and began gaining acceptance in shows and galleries. "These successes did a lot for me in transforming my painting from hobby to full-time career." When her daughter, Pua, graduated from high school, Pamela moved to Maui. "While living at the Horse Center near Makawao, I found myself painting on location every day. I also found myself growing in my art on Maui. On Oahu there are too may distractions."

Pamela enjoys a variety of media—oils, watercolors, pastels, collage, monoprints and "three-dimension" paper—but prefers oils. Her favorite subjects are old wooden shacks and people. Pamela also shares her talents with teaching and expects to be doing more of that in the years ahead. She taught a Spring session at the Honolulu Academy of Arts on painting on location and teaches a course on outdoor painting at the Hui Noeau.

Kaui, 28"x 32", Oil on Linen

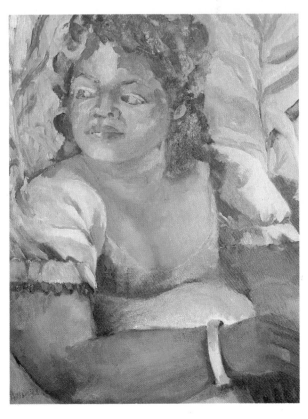

View from Swansons, 15" x 18", Private Collection

CENTRAL MAUI

THE HUB of government and commerce on Maui is shared by the towns of Wailuku and Kahului. Central Maui is largely these two towns, a mill at Puunene and acres of waving sugar cane. Wailuku, the old town and county seat, and Kahului, the new town and commercial center, are a study in contrasts. They are divided visually by a reef of sand left high and dry eons ago by the receding ocean.

In these sand hills the fearsome, tattooed Kahekili defeated the elite forces of the invading king of the Big Island, Kalaniopuu. At that time Kahekili, who ruled O'ahu, Maui, Moloka'i and Lana'i, had his Maui residence in Wailuku at the corner of present-day Main and High Streets (near the gas pumps of the police motorpool). The whole area surrounding high street belonged to the royal family of Maui. Kahekili's personal heiau remains beneath the foundation of Ka'ahumanu Church. Honolii Park at Main and High was an ancient and sacred burial ground for worthy alii, and the Bailey House (home of the Maui Historical Society) sits on "the best royal lands available" which were given to the missionaries for a school by Governor Hoapili in 1832. It is appropriate that the county and state governments of Maui reside here.

Wailuku is also the site of the first attempts to commercially refine sugar on Maui, and Hawaii's first railroad: a narrow gauge track two miles long built in 1880 to link the Wailuku mill with the port of Kahului. Being located in a pocket just removed enough from the beaches and commercial growth of Kahului to have been bypassed by the tourist boom, Wailuku has preserved many of the buildings and much of the appearance it had in the '40s and '50s. The old Grand Hotel and Wailuku Hotel, which housed military on leave and most visitors to Maui in those years, are gone. So too is the drug store on Market Street that served banana splits and green river. But the Iao Theatre, where Maui's youth spent Saturday afternoons at the matinee, still stands; and there is still a breadfruit tree on Main Street.

"All is takes is the two-mile drive down Main Street to neighboring Kahului to realize just how distinctively Hawaiian Wailuku really is..." writes Allen Seiden for *Aloha* magazine, June 1985. Kahului is a striking contrast with its modern shopping centers, community college, industrial area, housing tracts, and airport. With the development of the sugar industry came the construction of the harbor facilities at Kahului. And with the movement of labor off plantation camps came the housing that fans out across the plain from the harbor. During the war NASKA (Naval Air Station Kahului) was built eventually giving us the airport and light industrial area surrounding it. Only the Ka'naha' Pond Wildlife Sanctuary remains of the old ragged Hawaiian fishing village that was Kahului in ancient times.

The marsh-like appearance of the sanctuary camouflages its man-made origin. Two ponds were created about 270 years ago in the days of Kiha-a-piilani, then king of Maui. One story relates how the walls of the ponds were constructed by long lines of men imported from Moloka'i, who passed rocks hand-to-hand all the way from Maalaea. For many years the ponds contained primarily mullet. They were rededicated in the days of Kahekili by his younger son, Kamehameha-nui (not to be confused with Kamehameha the Great), and named Ka'naha' and Mauoli after the high prince Ka-hahana and his sister Kekela. Nature and man have reshaped the ponds over the years. They became closed to the sea and stagnant during the war and rechanneled after. Today the Ka'naha' Pond Wildlife Sanctuary is home and breeding ground for many of Hawaii's endangered birds and refuge for numerous migrant marsh and shore birds.

Through the port and airport of Kahului flow most of the goods and people in transit to and from Maui. The twice weekly appearance of Hawaii's "Loveboat," the S.S. *Oceanic Independence* is the latest steamship version of vessels like the *Hualalai,* and *Humuula* which carried passengers, freight and cattle in competition with inter-island schooners at the turn of the century. Of the two side-wheel river boats attempted in this service, one was wrecked off Kaua'i and the other wound up on a river in China. The last of the schooners was withdrawn in 1910 and by 1950 Kahului Railroad, the oldest rainroad in Hawaii, was handling almost all the aspects of transportation on the island, including a large fleet of trucks, and bus and school bus service, the stevedore service, the two steamship lines of Matson and Isthmian as well as the railroad.

Heading out along the coast beyond the airport is the small community of Spreckelsville, of whose gracious seaside homes many were destroyed in the tsunami (or tidal wave) that hit Maui in the early morning hours of April Fools' Day, 1946, The Maui Country Club (Maui's first golf course), Kaunoa (an elementary school at that time) and a few homes survived to combine with the slow growth that has taken place since. The stretch of coast from Spreckelsville through Paia heading outward has become a windsurfer's heaven, and is being repopulated by new arrivals seeking sun, sea and a rural setting.

MARTIN BANDY:

A Sailor's Pastime

THE ANCIENT FOLK ART OF ENGRAVING IVORY
OR SCRIMSHAW IS ALIVE AND WELL IN LAHAINA

Born in Southern California, Martin Bandy traversed a good part of the globe in the process of growing up. "I was really raised in Rome, with all of Europe for a back drop. My parents are both artists and I was always surrounded by great art. I took art when I was in high school in Italy." Martin returned to California to attend San Jose State and the University of California in Berkeley.

The young artist worked in varied art fields exploring oils, commercial and industrial art, even made some sculpture. He does some pen and ink and watercolor work still, mostly to help friends or for good

causes. He moved with his wife and three children to Maui in 1970, while he was working for Lockheed as an illustrator. Lockheed pulled out and Martin Bandy stayed. "I found my own little bit of paradise. For a creative artist with a love for history and the sea, Maui was the ideal place."

If Maui is the ideal place, scrimshaw, combining history and the sea as it does, is certainly the ideal medium. Martin's classical European background has allowed him to transform what used to be a sailor's pastime into a very fine art—preserving at the same time an endangered form of American Folk Art. Ivory in the form of sperm whale teeth

was readily available at the height of whaling and scrimshandling. Today a variety of ivories are used including fossilized ivory. The technique is basically that of dry point etching, using ivory instead of a metal plate.

"I sort of backed into it," says Martin. "A friend who was running a gift shop in Lahaina asked me if I could do some and provided a couple pieces of ivory." From there it has taken off and supported the Bandys ever since. Martin's approach and fascinating character studies in ivory have made their way to private collections throughout the world, coming to the attention of maritime galleries and museums in New England—the ancient birthplace of great whaling fleets.

Martin works out of his oceanside home with a view of the sea and his collection of nautical books. He says he remembers the portraits of Frans Hals, of the many masters he grew up with. "Some things stick. I also like the work of William Turner and the impressionists." Most of Martin's work can be seen in the Scrimshaw Factories of the old whaling capital of Lahaina.

Above: *Untitled (Captain and crew aboard a sailing barque, circa 1890), 6¾"x 3", Sperm Whale Tooth, Lahaina Scrimshaw Factory*
Below: *Untitled (Sailors stowing whale blubber aboard the Brig* Daisy *circa 1912), 9½"x 2¼", Fossilized Walrus Tusk, Lahaina Scrimshaw Factory*

ANDREW ANNENBERG:

With Singleness of Purpose

PAINTING TEACHES ME PATIENCE, A GLIMPSE OF THE
TIMELESSNESS FROM WHICH ALL EMERGES

Self-portrait, 8"x 10", Oil on Panel

Andrew Annenberg moved with his parents to Washington, D.C., when he was only nine months old. He remembers drawing continually from age seven, and an eye-opening, heart-shaping visit to the Smithsonian Institute. "I was so deeply touched by the great masterpieces there that the desire to create works of that level of excellence was born in me."

At age fifteen Andrew and his family returned to Santa Monica where he took up oils seriously and became the youngest member of the Santa Monica Art Association. "We showed our works in empty parking lots...anywhere to get exposure." At age twenty he moved to a classic garret paid for with an occasional painting. For awhile he

Dance of Life,
22"x 28", Oil,
Private Collection

The Illumined and Playful, 24"x 30", Oil, Private Collection

earned money stretching canvas and framing. Except for that, Andrew's whole time has been devoted to painting. "What else is there to do."

Andrew is a self-taught realist or surrealist whose education was given a great boost by a trip to Europe in the '60s. He also traveled to Nepal, Bali and Japan in 1981, "but the trip to Europe influenced my art the most." He moved to Maui in 1974 and remains inspired by the "exuberance of Nature's unique forms here: turquoise ocean, lava shores, volcanoes, waterfalls, pools, emerald jungles and flowers." As an artist working on Maui, he feels that the people, their "friendliness and

benevolence," are as important to him as the landscape.

Oils are Andrew's favorite medium. "I enjoy the luminosity and depth possible with oils. And there is nothing like a well-primed canvas. It has the softness and firmness of skin." He says, "Art is love made manifest," and it's clear from talking with him that his love extends to the tools of the trade.

"My art is my way to share the gift of consciousness that has been given me," Andrew says. "Painting teaches me patience, a glimpse of the timelessness from which all emerges."

Libra, 18"x 24", Oil on Panel, Private Collection

Daybreak Concerto, 16"x 20", Oil on Panel, Private Collection

JACKIE PIAS CARLIN:

Functional, Touchable Art

FABRIC PROVIDES AN UNUSUALLY GOOD OPPORTUNITY TO PRESERVE MY SENSE OF WHAT IS REAL HAWAII

Jackie works on the Kapalua Bay Project called Wisps, Acrylic on Cotton Blend,

Through the Dutch doors of a small studio shop in the Kahului Shopping Center called "Island Living," one may discover some of the most touchable fine art on the island. One may also meet Jackie Pias Carlin, the artist whose floral designs cover pillows, wall hangings and upholstery. The chances are that she will have a new project stretched out in some phase of assembly or creation; her small daughter Puacita helping in the back, and soft-spoken partner Jim Swor keeping track of the books.

Jackie has lived on Maui all her life, growing up in the plantation town of Paia where she remembers, "...hibiscus hedges, Ti leaf-bordered sidewalks and bird of paradise and other exotics growing along the roadsides." Her creative energies at this time were channeled into sewing and hula. This was followed by a professional singing career, which she pursued until she married her late husband, James Carlin. Together they launched into a very successful candlemaking business and singing became a sideline that Jackie still enjoys. Along the way Jackie dabbled in different fine art media and in 1976 began training with Don Roberts, using only charcoal—"...life drawing mostly"—until 1980 when she began two years of study with Gloria Foss. "This was a real turning point for me—everything seemed to click."

"I was happily expressing myself with oils, acrylics and pastels when I happened to stumble upon fabric painting. A friend, Paul Alexander, needed a line of handpainted silks for his interior design showroom." Supply and demand took over and opened a special career for this talented young artist. And the new art form opened avenues of expression as well. "I'm breaking barriers within my mind that were not possible in other media."

Jackie's style has been influenced by oriental and art nouveau methods. "Hisashi Otsuka, a master fabric painter, has been a great help to me. His insights have stuck and I recall his advice every now and then.... I

really enjoy what I'm doing, and I'm able to paint exactly what I want to say through this form." Jackie calls what she's doing "'Functional Art.' It takes the creative process a step further when the customer's environment, color preferences and feeling are all taken into consideration. And then the finished work is handled, touched—useful as well as decorative."

Jackie begins her design work with one or two sessions on location—"...sitting on a rock in midstream, or getting to know an orchid 6" away from its throat. I have never been able to work with photos, I need a better sense of the life within and around things." Jackie's research, sketches and notes, go through several stages evolving into designs for fabrics. "My tropical designs are easier to duplicate yard after yard because of the system I use. The free-style or abstract designs are more difficult."

Jackie's dream of doing large pieces of art is being realized with recent commissions of 66 yards of fabric for the Maui Country Club and 152 yards for the Kapalua Bay Hotel. "The upholstery designs are the most challenging and rewarding of the variety of things I'm doing."

Heat Wave, 25 yds x 54", Acrylic on 100% cotton canvas, Maui Country Club

Ti and Ike's Heliconia, Acrylic on 100% cotton canvas, 16"x 16" pillow and 33"x 54" wall hanging

Hong Kong Sampans, 16"x 20", Oil, Private Collection

JOYCE CLARK:

In Search of Fresh Seas

DOING MOSAICS MADE ME ACUTELY AWARE OF
THE INTERACTION OF SMALL FACETS OF COLOR

Seascape, 24"x 40", Oil, Private Collection

Beach Kids, 18"x 24", Oil, Private Collection

oyce Clark is one of Hawaii's premier artists, painting the islands since 1960 and making Maui her permanent home since 1970. "Hana is kind of hard to top. It's virgin territory, both intense and peaceful. Distance is only occasionally a problem and often a bonus. You see, I always carry my camera...I'm always looking, or seeing...there isn't any time that I'm not working, although work is probably the wrong word for it."

Joyce is herself an intense person, although "exuberant" is probably a better word. She was raised in the famous Art Colony of Laguna Beach, California and formally educated at Whittier College and the University of California at Los Angeles. Joyce then spent many years as a commercial artist and ceramic decorator.

Her first international recognition and acclaim came when Joyce was chosen in 1958 as one of two artists representing California in the first "ART:USA"show in Madison Square Garden in New York City. Her mosaics in California include a mural of St. Francis which graces the fascade of the St. Francis Hospital in Lynwood, "Future in Space," which hangs at Tulare High School, four symbolic murals in the Congregational Church in Laguna Beach and four tower murals in Leisure World at Laguna Beach.

"One of the most important events in my life was moving to Maui. It's affected my art in many of ways, increasing an awareness of light and shadow, more subtle and yet brilliant color. I feel my work has picked up a sense of freedom, warmth and spontaneity...a broader range of subjects..." Joyce has gotten away from the mosaics since moving to Hana. "I still carry designs in my head for

Outrigger, 20"x 30", Oil, Private Collection

mosaics I hope to complete one day. But I do oils almost exclusively now....the work with ceramic tile gave me an awareness of the interaction of small facets of color. I use that in my painting.

"Loving the ocean and living on an island surrounded by water is pure joy! I want my art to reflect that joy and more." Joyce is a "water-oriented, seascape specialist," who has traveled extensively along the coasts of California, Oregon, Mexico and Hawaii as well as the islands of the South Pacific, Arizona, Alaska, Egypt and throughout mainland China. "The trips keep me fresh. I'm going back to China, there's so much to see there."

Joyce admires the work of Dick Nelson, George Allan, Lowell Mapes and Honolulu artists Lao Chun and Tagami but feels she has learned more from her own disciplined efforts than from the work of other artists. "We learn from doing. I think it's the only way." Her works may be seen currently at the Village Galleries on Maui or by appointment in her studio.

Obaki, 13" x 18", Watercolor

CYNTHIA CONRAD:

A Touch of Wit and Humor

THE NEXT BEST THING IS SURPRISING THE AUDIENCE
WITH AN UNEXPECTED POINT OF VIEW OR SUBJECT

A painter in the realistic tradition, Cynthia Conrad was born in the San Francisco Bay area and graduated from the University of California, Berkeley campus, with a B.A. in painting. "When I was six, my aunt showed me how to draw faces and I have a special feeling for her. She was a major influence in my life as an artist."

Throughout grade school, junior high and high school, Cynthia was the class artist, gaining an art scholarship upon graduation. At Berkeley she was immersed in the total dawn-to-candle-light life of an artist. The university in the late '60s surrounded Cynthia with some of the best in the business. "I was fortunate to be able to study under R. B. Kitah, Felix Ruvulo, David Simpson, Ron Nagel, Alex Katz, Peter Voulkos, Elmer Bischoff and many others."

Cynthia moved to Maui in 1970 where she works as an art director in advertising. "The beauty of Maui is what influences my work now...the quality of light, the saturation of color and the endless array of timeless and classic subject matter."

Although she has worked with oils and acrylics, Cynthia prefers large watercolors and works almost exclusively in this medium. She enjoys contemporary representational art and likes to call what she does "synthesized reality," because it "copies life but has the odd perspective." Certainly a part of the wit and humor she tries to include in her work is gained by her love of the unusual composition.

"The best part of painting is the actual laying down of the paint. For me it is a transcendental experience, when the work takes on a life of its own. The next thing is surprising the audience with an unexpected point of view or subject. I have a feeling for what will catch the viewer's interest and if the allusion is to something funny or sexy I know I can evoke an emotion. The primal references to childhood or even a simple depiction of lush or soothing beauty will also cause a click of recognition. I know what excites me and I trust it will stimulate others. I want my paintings to heal, to please, to seduce."

Happy Bird,
24"x 32",
Watercolor

SIDNEY T.K. YEE:

The Soft-Spoken Ceramist

ONE IS CONSTANTLY DEALING WITH THE EFFECTS OF
ABSTRACT QUALITIES OF SHAPE, TEXTURE, COLOR

Kiawe Kapu, 18" high

When I was growing up," said Sidney, "nobody figured art was anything serious. To get ahead you went into law, medicine or business. That feeling is still there among lots of local families."

Sidney T.K. Yee grew up in Waipahu, Oahu, and went on to the University of Hawaii to pursue a career in architecture. "I sort of backed into what I'm doing now. My interests were always in the designing area. So when I shifted to education, I went into art education and took a lot of art courses....ceramics came naturally to me. I find it easier to deal with the abstract qualities rather than with representational art." Sidney came out of the University of Hawaii with a master's degree in secondary art education. In his last year at the university, he married a Maui girl, which helped bring him to this island eventually.

Before moving however, Sidney taught for five years at Leilehua. "I moved to Maui in 1975 seeking a slower pace." He has been running an art program at Lahainaluna and working out of his father-in-law's storeroom ever since. "When he [Sidney's father-in-law] stopped raising honeybees, he let me use the whole area." Sidney makes use of two good-sized kilns: gas for the raku work, and electric for ware such as tiles which require an even heat throughout.

"I fool around with stoneware, but for the galleries it's all raku....Toshiko Takaezu

Mokuaweoweo, 1"x 14"

influenced me a lot early in my career. When I saw the beautiful rounded shapes she was creating it set a pattern. For a long time I did just rounded shapes. I've also admired the work of David Kuraoka and Randy Hokushin. I liked watching the progression of Hokushin's work from show to show." Recently Sidney has begun to expand into representational art and other media, pastels and airbrush especially. "It's kind of an extension of both areas, the teaching and the pottery."

A recent commission from the Hawaii State Foundation On Culture And The Arts fills much of Sidney's studio space at the moment. The work in two parts—both in progress—includes a ceramic tile mural and a wood and cement sculpture for the Hana Library. "The theme, a Hawaiian trinity of gods, 'Kaua ka kahi,' has forced me into dealing with images again. It's part of my new explorations."

Sidney is a quiet, soft-spoken artist who tries to achieve, through his pottery, statements that reflect the spirit of raku, "its harmony, peace and tranquility."

KIHEI

KIHEI WAS A store and a few beach cottages, then came a kiawe and cactus wasteland, a sand and dirt washboard road highlighted by a fishing cove and concrete bunkers built by the Marines, until you reached Eddie Chang's pig farm and Makena landing. Harold Rice had hives and a bee run in the kiawes behind Kiawekapu (between Kihei and Wailea). Kihei was a dusty sneeze on the two-hour ride to what is now Polo Beach, where as kids we spent weekends climbing the sprawling kiawes and swimming or fishing. It wasn't always like that, and it is certainly not like that today.

When Captain John Joseph Halstead set up a trading center in Kihei more than 100 years ago, the area was fertile agricultural land. The Hawaiian village of Kalepolepo sprawled across the nine-mile-long Kihei beach, where the Hawaiians grew coconut and taro and maintained a fishpond they called Ko'ie'ie. Halstead was a sea captain from New York who serviced the whaling fleet that worked the waters off Maalaea. He built a three-story Pennsylvania Dutch farm house and almost all the furnishings out of koa wood. The "Koa House," with a store on the ground floor, became the gathering place for the entire coast and visiting spot for Hawaiian royalty. Kings Kamehameha III, Kamehameha IV, Kamehameha V and Lunalilo, all spent time with the sea captain and his Koa House.

With the decline of whaling during the 1870s came the eclipse of Halstead's business. In 1876 he closed his store and moved to Ulupalakua, where he died in 1887. His Koa House, however, survived another half century before being condemned and burned. In 1890 the then Territory of Hawaii chose Maalaea Bay for a boat landing, and Kihei Pier was constructed near the present junction of old Kihei Road and Puunene Highway. For many years inter-island boats landed freight at and shipped produce from Kihei Pier. The sugar train connected central Maui across the neck for transportation of goods and people. Subsequently landings were constructed at Makena and Keawapau, further south on the coast. Passengers and cargo also were discharged at Lahaina, but that was a small boat-to-shore operation. Kihei Pier operated until around 1915 when the area sanded in to such an extent that it became impossible for vessels to reach the pier.

By this time the old village of Kalepolepo was gone. The earlier sandlewood trade and subsequent timbering had denuded the slopes of Haleakala. The resulting soil runoffs carved the mountain slopes, silted in the fishpond and transformed Kalepolepo into a dusty desert. And with the economic shifts, Hawaiian families drifted away. For a time in the late 1800s, after his government service, David Malo, famed native historian, was pastor of the Kalepolepo church. Today Trinity By The Sea holds Sunday services in the kiawe embraced ruins.

In the quiet years before statehood and the flood of new faces, Kihei was home to a few fishermen and roaming cattle. The small Kihei bridge, called Charley Young Bridge, was named after the noted writer for *The Maui News* who bought a piece of Kihei in 1940. The Marines invaded during the war, built imitations of Japanese concrete bunkers, seeded the surf with steel rod and concrete landing-craft mines and conducted training maneuvers. In 1950 Bill Azeka opened a small grocery store along the dusty Kihei Road. Today Azeka Place is a complex of 38 stores and shops and Bill is known as "the honorary mayor of Kihei." A great variety of local people built beach cottages during the '50s, farmers dug wells and a school was built. Then with the land boom people came from everywhere to stake their claims to a chunk of sand.

Today Kihei is a bustling hodgepodge of shops, condominiums and homes which pay tribute to the pioneering and entrepreneurship of "little guys." It is the great unplanned development on Maui with all the character—and characters—that a total cross section of Hawaii will give you. More than 5,000 people call it home, and hundreds more swell its ranks every winter. The kiawe trees still prosper along with cactus, but the road has been paved and a thriving and colorful community is well established.

Just beyond Kihei and Kiawekapu is the giant Wailea development with its two hotels, fine dining restaurants, tennis courts and golf courses—a beautifully planned and pristine contrast to the ragged and more lively Kihei. In the early stages of this development an art center was planned with dreams of a great art colony developing. And while this has not yet come to pass, Kihei has attracted a fair share of talent and developed a small art community of its own.

HAJIME OKUDA:

A Half-Century Pilgrimage

"IN A WHOLE LIFETIME, THAT IDEA [OF BEING AN ARTIST] DOESN'T RUN AWAY FROM YOUR HEAD,"

When I was 16 I told my friends, 'I'm going to Hawaii to study art.' But when I came here I cannot do what I like. I have to work." And work the young Hajime Okuda did. In his teens he was a "printer's devil," "picking up words" that were cast in lead type at the *Hawaii Times* and *Hawaii Hochi* before switching to the spoken word and narrating silent Japanese films. He met and married a local girl on Maui while doing "mo'om picture" house gigs and settled in Wailuku. The Okudas had seven daughters over the years before Hajime could "get ahead" enough to become a full-time art student. "I was with the moving picture business until the war began. After the war started...I got a job in sugar."

During World War II, Hajime augmented his 45-cents-an-hour plantation job by making block print designs for marines stationed on Maui. Soon he was making

Below: *Lanai Sunset, 36"x 48", Oil, Private Collection*
Next page: *Pioneer Mill, 17"x 30", Oil*

$2,000-a-month selling scarfs, muumuus, table cloths, napkins and "ladies' clothes." With that capital, in 1946 he started the H. Okuda grocery store in Wailuku.

Three years later Hajime built the first supermarket on Maui. After a full day serving customers, he would sleep some and get up at 2 a.m. to paint. His first major projects were two 30-foot by six-foot murals (an underwater scene and a landscape) for the walls of his market. "Every week I painted my promotion ads on the market windows—cigarettes, coffee, whatever was on sale that week. I used water paints, washed 'em off with a big hose, then painted the new one for next week."

In 1958, after numerous diversions and with a successful business in hand, Hajime Okuda decided the time had come to pursue his real goal. "I was 52 years old. I told my wife, Oshino, I better quit and do painting, what I wanted to do all my life. She said all right. She always said 'all right' to what I think.... My wife and I and three daughters moved to Honolulu and I started studying at the Honolulu Academy of Arts and University of Hawaii night classes. I learned from plenty people—John Young, Wilson Stamper, Peter Hayward, Joe Ferrer.

"The first three years I didn't sell anything. Just painting, trying hard. Then in 1961 I won first prize in the Association of Honolulu Artists show." With this start his work began to sell and Hajime returned to Japan to study art. His plans to study in Paris fell through so he returned to Hawaii to paint scenes he had lived with for more than half a lifetime.

The above is largely a rewrite of an article by Mary Cooke which appeared in the *Honolulu Advertiser* Monday, March 25, 1974. Hajime Okuda is 79 years old as of this writing and still painting most everyday. His work can be seen in many of the banks in Honolulu and Maui, as well as at galleries in Lahaina and the Pacific Gallery in Honolulu.

JOHN BARDWELL:

Island is Friendly to Artists

THE REARRANGEMENT OF SHAPES AND COLORS LIFTING SUBJECTS OUT OF CONTEXT FOR A FRESH VIEW

Papaya Afternoon, 18"x 24", Water-color, Private Collection

After 20-odd years, I still think that painting pictures is a strange way to make a living," said John Bardwell, one of the growing corps of professional artists who discovered Maui while vacationing from their mainland jobs. John spent a dozen previous years in the deserts and mountains of Nevada.

"This island is friendly to artists. You can say without hesitation that you are a full time artist or craftsman. You can even put it on a credit application without fear of automatic rejection." John grew up in southern California and graduated from the Art Center College of Design. He was doing commercial design and illustration in his second year of school and the day after graduation in 1965, he opened his own design studio in Hollywood.

"I was looking forward to a long and very

profitable career in the glamour world of corporate design and advertising. But as time passed, business became less fulfilling and I knew it was necessary to return to basics. Art is still pretty pure. Sure, there are always people who try to corrupt art for the big money, but you'll find them in every field."

Although he is not verbal about his own work, John readily shares his feelings about the nature and condition of art and the art market. In conversation, you are not surprised to learn that Bardwell is also a professional writer and understands modern communication technique.

"I feel there is still integrity in art. It is harder to find integrity in government or business. There is less honesty in personal relationships—a marked difference over just one generation. A lot of art 'experts' try to define a painting or sculpture with obscure words which mean very little to me. They do this I think because they're in love with words or need to justify their jobs. In the end it's the artwork itself that speaks or fails to."

Bardwell admits that his views are not popular in some corners of the art world. "I would rather see people admire and buy art they like or can identify with—that touches something inside them—than buying art as an investment.

"My work with watercolors is almost or semi realistic. It's influenced by what the impressionists and abstract artists have done. But basically I rearrange shapes and colors—take subject matter out of context to show it in a different frame of reference."

Koi Pond, 18"x 24", Watercolor

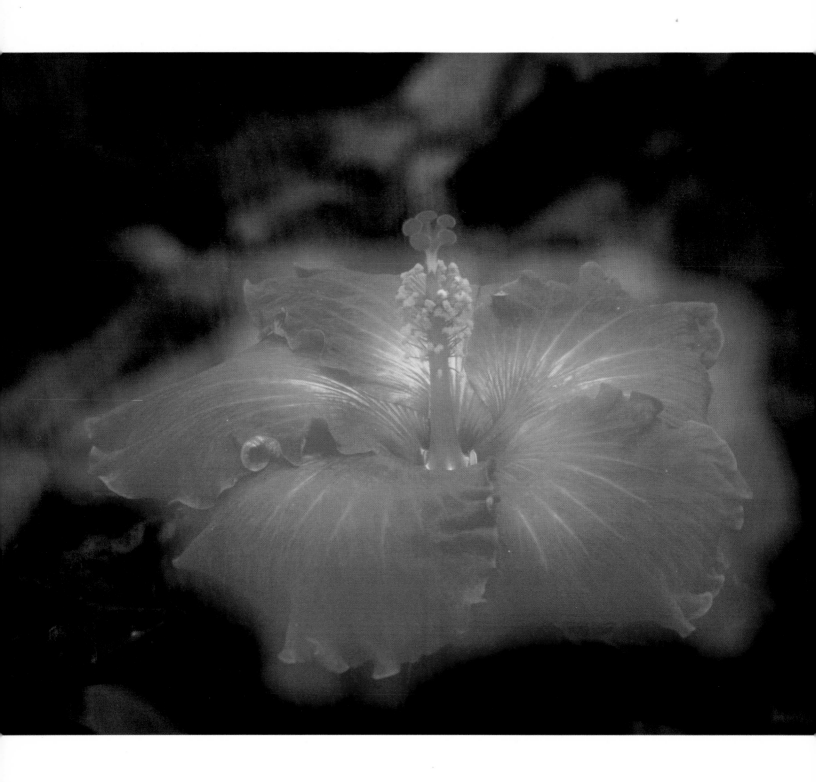

RUSSELL BEACH:

Under a Full Moon

NEARLY HALF THE CREATIVE WORK OF ALL FINE ART
PHOTOGRAPHY TAKES PLACE IN THE DARKROOM

My photographs most often result from ideas that come to mind at strange hours of the night," says Russell Beach, who usually pre-visualizes his images completely. "A gallery in the mind, so to speak, because I clearly see the image with all its subtleties down to the matte and frame." This does not preclude recording the chance image when it is discovered, and Russ, like so many other artists, travels with camera against just such a chance. However,

he finds that the challenges of photography are greatly increased when attempting to reproduce a preconceived image.

Russ was born and grew up in the Mid-West, moving to Santa Barbara, California to acquire his photographic training at Brook's Institute of Photography. "I took up photography when I discovered it went a long way to satisfying an all consuming wonderlust!" Some of that wonderlust has been satiated by a career that has taken Russ to more than 30 countries including Europe, Asia, Africa and the Arctic.

Throughout most of this odyssey, Russ has specialized in scientific and research photography, working at such places as the White Sands Missile Range, the National Center for Atmospheric Research, the Geophysical Institute at the University of Alaska and presently for the AVCO Everett Research Laboratory on Maui. "My long association with scientific and technical photography has provided me with an increased knowledge of the possibilities that the photographic medium can achieve. A thorough understanding of good technique can liberate one's creative urges.

"Living and working on Maui has allowed me to become acquainted with a broad range of cultures and ethnic groups working

together.... This has had greater impact on me than all the other aspects of Maui's great beauty." Working for AVCO has been a special plus for Russ as this company encourages and supports his experimentation, research, and artful pursuits. These he has been able to share with the community through his association with Maui Community College, where he has been teaching color photography for the past ten years.

Russ feels very strongly that the photographers who present their work as art must have carried the work entirely from exposure to final print. "Nearly half of all fine art photography takes place in the darkroom, and no photographer has the right to call a work their own unless they have, at the very least, personally prepared a master print from which any other print has been created." It is this very technical expertise that gives wings to the photography of Russell Beach.

YOSHIKO FUJITA:

Bohemian Free Spirit

BUT WHEN I PAINTED, ALL MY PROBLEMS DISAPPEARED. I THOUGHT OF NOTHING BUT ART

An original. A self-creation standing there in a longish, black dress that drapes in front, held with an oversized antique brooch. The face is intense and pale. The lips vermillion. And the head, a black mass of hair atop which sets a neat little hat with a puff on one side and a swath of black dotted net across the face." Kaui Goring, *The Maui News* feature article, October 14, 1984.

Yoshiko Fujita had a comfortable childhood, growing up as part of a wealthy

Sustenance of Life, 20"x 24", Oil

Elegance, 16"x 22", Oil

family outside Kyoto, Japan. By age 17, however, she had come to hate the pointlessness of her existence and the predictability of its future. So she ran away to Manchuria taking her maid and wandered for a year. Eventually her maid fell in love and deserted her, and then the money ran out. "I didn't know what I wanted from this world, now I know."

Back in Japan a year later disguised as a Korean, which fooled no one, she was quickly picked up and returned to her family. And while her family strove to interest her in a better way of life, even giving her schooling in art and design, Yoshiko strove to "walk around in the streets with barefeet....I didn't yet know what things were important. Now I know, they are art and religion." She worked as a fashion model for awhile, made a few pre-war (WWII) movies, spent time as a theatrical designer and tried several marriages. "But when I painted, all my

problems disappeared. I thought of nothing but art."

In 1955, married to an American military officer, Yoshiko and her young son, who is now a pilot, moved to the West Coast. Yoshiko is quite proud of having put her son through school with her art. On the West Coast, she studied at the Schneider Art Institute in Los Angeles, the San Francisco Art Institute and spent time with Maria Rubenstein. She also spent some time in Europe studying with Fredrik Goldburg in Germany and Thomas Lyton in England.

An unusual life and an intense drive to rise above the ordinary has given Yoshiko and her work a keen sense of drama. She followed her son to Maui and now lives, paints and conducts classes on the island. Traditional, realistic and occasionally somber, her work displays a painterly touch combined with a lively concern for the play of light.

Fanning the Nights as Hot as Lava, 18"x 23", Acrylic on masonite, ceramic and copper,
Private Collection

WILL HERRERA:

Symbols and Social Comment

THERE ARE TECHNICAL HANDICAPS FOR A SCULPTOR ON MAUI
HOWEVER HEALING AND INSPIRATION ARE NOT AMONG THEM

I would be working in my studio," Will Herrera related, "and the next thing I knew, I was outside weeding the garden or trimming trees or landscaping. Maui's wonderful sensual environment is so alluring that it does that for me. We've lost a good number of artists to windsurfing and the like." And for Will, Maui provides continual inspiration and the raw material for his castings. Real creatures, plants and various objects such as rocks and roots are all grist for his symbol-making process. "I do have to travel to the mainland for two- or three-week spells every now and then. There are no foundries here and I like to keep up with technical advancements."

Born in Los Angeles, Will began painting in 1967 and within a year expanded to include ceramic and metal sculpture. It is for his ceramic sculpture that Will Herrera has gained outstanding worldwide recognition. Will studied at California State University at Northridge, Santa Barbara Art Institute and California State College in Sonoma as well as receiving a graduate student invitation to study at the University of Southern California in Los Angeles. Will moved to Maui in 1976 where he works out of a studio in Kihei.

"I feel the need to say something in my art about the conditions in which we live, the problems of our time—acid rain, the bombing of Kaho'olawe, violence…such work doesn't really sell well. People like the purely decorative art." And yet it was the sale of just such a piece that paid for Will's first trip to Hawaii. The highly detailed clay sculpture, a commentary on war and peace, was purchased by the Peace Action Council in 1968. His more commercially successful statements can be appreciated on many levels with the social comment riding quietly beneath the surface. "Kala Atomica," for example, is such a fine piece of work technically and design wise that the significance of the choice of elements could easily be missed, or even interpreted in different ways. In this piece the artist has combined a porcelain casting of a lava rock, a machine precise triangle and the colorful unicorn fish called "Kala" to make a statement about the bombing of Kaho'olawe. It poses on a larger scale the whole question of man's relationship to nature. Or, if you choose, you may simply enjoy the marvelous interaction of space, color and form.

"Fanning the Nights as Hot as Lava" moves in an entirely different direction. In this exploration of mixed media relief and resulting serigraph print, Will intends to provoke a sense of timeless splendor, "a brief vacation of sorts from the realities of the world today." The title is a reference to the artist's creative process which Will has coined "research in spontaneous achievement."

Next page: *Lady Deco, 7′x 3′x 4′, Bronze with silver patina on lacquered wood base (photo: Michael Miller)*

Kala Atomica, 20″x 21″x 10″, Porcelain, low fire clay, glazes, platinum and gold fired on surface, Private Collection (photo: Steve Minkowski)

WEST MAUI

IN MAY OF 1962, only seven months before the opening of the first hotel at Kaanapali, Bob Krauss commented in the *Honolulu Advertiser* on the "march of progress" in Lahaina with a few words on the opening of a brand new laundromat. "This laundromat used to be a carport. It has no door, no windows. In fact, it doesn't even have walls, just a roof. Here, fronting a narrow alley, the rows of automatic washers sit in the sunshine amongst the banana trees.... Housewives in muumuus have turned the place into a social center. They bring their guitars and ukuleles. While the machines are churning, the tutus chat and sing away the time.

"The other day a woman with two small children brought them and a bundle of laundry to the new laundromat. She undressed the kids and stuffed the clothes in to wash. Part of the soap she brought with her went into the machine. The rest of it went on the kids who she stuck under a faucet and scrubbed while the week's washing was being done. When the load was finished, she dressed the kids in their clean clothes, tucked the clean laundry under her arm and marched home."

This picture of the sleepy village of Lahaina coming out of a period when poi and fish were still the staple commodities and the "action" was elsewhere has drawn tourists by the thousands. This is not really the Lahaina they discover when they arrive and yet they will return year after year for the drama, vitality and turn-of-the-century charm that marks this former whaling port today. They come to stay at the resorts and condominiums that span the coast from Kaanapali and Kapalua, to enjoy the golf, tennis, quaint little sugarcane train, fine restaurants, the sun and sea. And while the sleepy village is no longer in evidence its casual way of life is clung to tenaciously.

The hot, dusty, small-town Lahaina that I remember was valid only for the hundred-year period she fell out of history. Being bypassed by Hawaii's modern history helped preserve the landmarks and architecture of the time when Lahaina was capital of the Hawaiian Kingdom and center of the whaling industry in the Pacific. Lahaina remained a backwater mill town just long enough for the historical and conservation consciousness of Maui to awaken and take action to preserve as much of the old flavor as possible. The first comprehensive historical restoration and preservation plan was published in 1961. And in 1962 (along with the opening of a new laundromat) Lahaina was designated a National Historic District. The Kaanapali Beach Resort was officially opened in December of 1962, and the Sheraton Maui in January of 1963. Since that time Lahaina has grown in character more and more like the dramatic center of action that it was in the heyday of whaling.

Today Lahaina is the focus of West Maui, an area extending from Olowalu on the south to Kapalua on the north. It has been said that without this hurly-burly Front Street and jumble of boutiques, restaurants and bars, Kaanapali is just another first-class resort area. Lahaina is where all the conflicting elements come together and are held in tenuous balance as they were in the 1800s when Lahaina was where Hawaii met the rest of the world.

In those days the young kingdom was struggling to create and preserve its identity in a world ready to swallow it up. Traders and speculators were trying to gain a foothold. Sailors were looking for a good time and missionaries were missionaries, both helping and hindering in an effort to save and teach and heal. Today the diverse elements of sugar, visitors, entrepreneurs, drifters who haven't decided what to do with their lives, the locals of all nationalities, entertainers and boat enthusiasts, investors and historians, find an uneasy truce in the colorful community where greed and the old aloha ethics battle daily. Lahaina is alive. One can find both the historic Baldwin House and Burger King™ on Front Street across from the largest banyan tree in the islands. Lahaina is once again the place where old Hawaii meets the rest of the world and chooses to walk forward as best it can. It is also the place where most of the artists of Maui exhibit their work.

As Lahaina started to awaken from its hundred-year slumber, Alexandra Morrow encountered artist Joyce Clark on Front Street with the question: "How do you go about starting an art society?" The Lahaina Arts Society—helping young artists, providing gallery space in the old court house, giving lessons and scholarships—was started in 1965. The running of the society's activities and maintenance of its facilities are entirely voluntary. The result is that most of the artists of Maui have been involved with this group at one time or another, giving of their time and talent: many owe their careers to its support.

(Continued on page 77)

Born in Melbourne, Australia, George Allan studied design at Melbourne Institute of Technology before setting off to study the world's art. He traveled for twelve years throughout the South Pacific, North and South America, Europe and Russia. "Austria became homebase for ten of those years. I was skiing mostly, and absorbing art wherever I could find it." George also spent a couple of years in London during this period. "Monet, Toulouse Lautrec are among my favorites...I was in awe of the impressionists."

"When I agreed in Denmark to help sail the *Carthaginian II* to Lahaina, I considered myself European. Europe was where things were happening." In 1973, four months after he set out, George arrived in Lahaina where he was immediately drawn into involvement with the Lahaina Arts Society. "I thought I'd stay for a few weeks, but I kept getting more involved. Then I started to grow as an artist. Where in Europe I was absorbing, here I began expressing what I had absorbed. The images, people and landscapes, were fresh and rich in diversity." George married a year and a half after arriving and has lived and worked in Lahaina ever since.

George still travels finding renewal and fresh images. "I've stopped taking as many photographs. It interferes with the experience of where you are. I can't use a photo anyway without a broader sense of the place. Back home looking at a photo, I want to associate people and events, sounds and smells. If I spent all the time behind a camera there are

Endless Spring Series VI, 25"x 35", Oil, Private Collection

GEORGE ALLAN:

You Never Stop Composing

I HADN'T THE SLIGHTEST INTENTION OF COMING
TO HAWAII, OR STAYING WHEN I DID COME

The Nuage,
34"x 50", Oil,
Private Collection

no associations, the picture is empty."

Back home, George was in the process of building a new studio when I talked to him. In this studio he is building a pit for his easels so he can work on much larger paintings. "I've always been impressed by large scale work. My paintings so far have been about two feet by three feet, which is comfortable for me. I've done a few slightly larger things, but always restricted by the space I have to work in. There is a danger in

working on a grand scale. A really large piece needs a large idea. One can't just paint big for the sake of painting big.

"I guess I don't have a particular message or philosophy in what I do. But I'm always on the alert for different ways of looking at things. Wherever I am, I'm composing pictures in my head. And every once in awhile I hit on something that must be painted. That's when art is fun—the spark, the initial idea."

Beach Picnic, 16"x 24", Oil, Private Collection

BILL BAGLEY:

Shapechanger with a Brush

IN ORDER TO BE HAPPY WITH MY WORK I HAVE TO BE
CONSTANTLY CHANGING STYLE AND TRYING NEW IDEAS

I guess I've always been an artist," said Bill Bagley during an interview. "I recall entering a drawing contest on a national television network when I was nine and winning first prize, a bicycle. But for years I didn't take my painting seriously even though my friends and family were always encouraging me to."

After studying art at the universities of New Hampshire and Vienna, Bagley took a break from art and pursued careers in teaching, counseling, carpentry and music, as well as running an outward bound program and owning and managing a couple of small businesses. He has traveled extensively, living in Mexico, Saint Thomas and in Bolivia with the Peace Corps.

*Kaanapali,
50"x 32", Oil on
Linen, Private
Collection*

White Ginger, 75"x 42", Oil, Private Collection

"Sometimes," said the artist, "it seems that I've done just about everything. At one point I decided to try my hand at homesteading and built a house in the Maine woods. But after six years of living without electricity and being occupied with cutting firewood and raising animals and vegetables, I decided that it was time to get back to my art, and in the summer of 1980 I made a decision to dedicate myself to my painting career."

Since then Bagley has had one-man shows in Massachusetts, Florida and Hawaii, and has participated in numerous group and juried shows. He has received much acclaim, particularly for his large, brilliantly colored florals and landscapes, although he is equally at ease doing figures or abstracts. It is difficult to categorize his paintings because of their seemingly limitless scope and diversity. "I don't like to be classified as a realist, an impressionist, or an abstract painter," Bill said. "To me art is an experimental and developmental process. In order to be happy with my work I have to be constantly changing and trying out new ideas."

Bill does several shows a year at this writing and tries to introduce a new theme or style each time. "But that doesn't look like a Bagley" is a common reaction of patrons returning for more of his work. He hopes that this idea of constantly exploring new directions will become an accepted identity marker rather than the more restricting labels most artists acquire. "It's not easy. People, dealers and customers, like to think they know your work and can predict the sort of thing you will do."

Bagley's surprising use of color goes back in part to his days in the Peace Corps. South America exposed him to different, bolder, perhaps more primitive use of color, especially primaries. "Seeing this work gave me a new sense or awareness of color. It expanded my frame of reference a great deal, and I guess I like to do that for the viewers of my work.

"Being on Maui does two really important things for me as an artist. First of all the physical environment, with its intense and dramatic shifts of color and form, is incredibly stimulating. And second, on the more practical side, there is international exposure here through the tourists. My work has done well commercially and there's that push—deadlines—which really helps."

Napili Coast Series I, 48"x 40", Oil, Private Collection

In the days of Kiha-a-Piilani, a great road was constructed to encircle the island. Smooth ocean stones handed from man to man were carefully fitted in place, the flatter stones on steeper ground—for walking ease while climbing and water run-off to prevent the stones from washing out. It was a joint venture that included the help of Umi, a chief from Hawaii who controlled the Hana district. The celebrated route was first called the Alaloa and later known as Kiha-a-Piilani Highway. Today the Honoapiilani Highway, the West Maui belt road, echoes that great achievement. Tradition has it that Kiha-a-Piilani's third child, Kihawahine, was buried in Lahaina beneath the small island of Moku-ula in the pond called Mokuhinia. She was deified as a mo'o (lizard or dragon), the one sacred being that unified the bloodlines of all inhabitants.

The small pond that is now a public recreation area disappeared when Pioneer Mill redirected the flow of water to irrigate cane fields. During the early days of the kingdom, the royal and sacred islet of Moku-ula (in this pond) supported two sophisticated grass houses with glass windows and a royal mausoleum. The kings Kamehameha II and III lived here during their reigns. Actually all three children of Kamehameha the Great and Queen Keopuolani (who, in the old system, outranked Kamehameha) were born in Lahaina and called it home. This seaside village was the capital of the island kingdom and center of Hawaiian government from the death of Kamehameha in 1819 to 1845, when the capital was moved to Honolulu. It was in 1819 that the first American whaleships, the *Equator* from Nantucket and *Balaena* from New Bedford, visited the Hawaiian Islands.

Here in the frothy clash of very different cultures Hawaii gots its first edict of religious tolerance, first bill of rights, first constitution, first legislature. The Pacific got the oldest high school west of the Rockies in 1831 (to which the folks of the California gold rush sent their children). And the Lahainaluna Seminary, as it was called then, produced the first native-Hawaiian scholar in David Malo. Malo was a constant advisor of kings, helped draft the 1840 constitution, and was outspoken on the threat posed by the flood of newcomers. His *Hawaiian Antiquities* is still read today, a century after his death.

In 1846 over 400 ships came to Maui and the census taken by the missionaries that year showed a Lahaina population of 3,557. There were 882 grass houses, 155 adobe houses, 59 of stone or wood and 528 dogs and 600 seamen. In 1851 the Rev. Henry Cheever wrote that "Lahaina is one of those places which you like much better as you approach or recede from it, than when you are actually in it. A little way off it seems sweetly embosomed in breadfruit trees, and all fresh and lovely with sunshine and verdure, calmly enclosed seaward within a fence of foam, made by the sea breaking upon the coral reef. Ride over the rollers in a whale-boat or native canoe, get to the sunburnt, dusty land, walk up a few rods, perhaps with pantaloons, to the mission houses, and make acquaintance on the way to your heart's content with Lahaina dust and caloric, and you will probably by that time be saying to yourself, 'Twas distance lent enchantment to the view.'"*

"'Twas" the "Lahaina Roads" that drew the traders and whalers. This open roadstead that stretches seven miles across to Lanai is on the lee side of West Maui Mountains and protected by neighboring islands. It meant 350 days a year of safe anchorage, no fee charged, and the ability to come and go on any wind that blew. Today the anchorage draws sailors on around-the-world (or Pacific) trips, sleek ketches from the bi-annual Victoria B.C. to Maui Yacht Race, work boats (fishermen and black coral divers) and charter boats of all types. And the waters on the lee side of Maui from Makena to Kaanapali draw the humpback whale in season to breed and play.

---

*Hawaii, Insight Guides, Apa Productions (Hong Kong) Ltd. 1980, pp. 245, 246.

A Gift To A Friend, Watercolor

GUY BUFFET:

A Frenchman in Lahaina

EACH PAINTING IS AN INVITATION TO BE HAPPY
I WANT YOU TO BE COMFORTABLE AND RELAXED

I am not trying," said Guy Buffet, "to convey a message in my work. Instead each painting is an invitation to a world where my dreams and fantasies become reality." Over the years Lahaina has seen its share of international figures. Guy Buffet has perhaps stayed around longer than most, endeavoring in his own unique fashion to explore and capture its flavor. Born in Paris in 1943, this French artist has been painting since he was a small child. At age 14 he left public school to study advanced art and design at the Academie de la Ville in Paris. At 19 he joined the French Navy; and it was through that navy that Guy (pronounced Gy) Buffet's paintings received their first international exposure.

On one of many exhibitions organized by the French Navy, Buffet was introduced to the Hawaiian Islands, and in 1963 he decided

Lahaina: The Pioneer Inn, Watercolor

Ice Tea By The Sea, 30"x 40", Acrylic

to make his home in the state he describes as "Paradise." Fascinated by the folklore and history of the islands, Buffet created a series of paintings depicting Hawaiian people and events. An early work featuring Captain Cook's arrival in Hawaii brought Buffet notoriety, and his career began to blossom.

With works exhibited in the permanent collections of the French Navy, the French Department of Foreign Affairs, and the museum of the French Navy, Buffet settled into a style of primitive folk-art, using acrylic and watercolors and his own impressionist technique. Buffet was awarded three major commissions from the Hawaii State Foundation On Culture And The Arts. He also painted murals for the Kaimuki Library in Honolulu, and the Community School Library in Waimanalo, Oahu.

Buffet's work was especially influenced by the island's many carnation fields. "Looking at them under the trade winds is just incredible," he says. "A great rainbow explodes before my eyes."

An extensive world traveler, Buffet was a guest of the Peking Arts and Crafts Council where he painted a series called "Guy Buffet's China." And drawing upon the experience, color and flavor of Hawaiian culture, he is working on a series of paintings depicting the wine country and great chefs of France.

"I invite the viewer to share my experience," says the artist, "I take you into my world like a guest into my home. I want you to be comfortable, relaxed, happy: to forget about problems and sorrows. If you like it and want to come back, my world is yours..."

Hana: Tiny, Watercolor

LARRY DOTSON:

Painting to Feed the Family

ARRIVING ON MAUI, THE FIRST THING I HAD TO DO WAS
GO OUT AND BUY TUBES OF COLOR—EXPAND THE PALETTE

"I was painting, teaching oils, and running a framing business on the West Coast," said Larry Dotson, "when the lure of Hawaii caught up with me and my family. We were importing matting and framing material from the Philippines and supplying hotels in Honolulu. We were looking for a less hectic pace." Larry has discovered that living and working in Lahaina not only provides him and his family with a more relaxed and informal lifestyle, but also a wider range of subjects to paint and a ready market among the many visitors and galleries.

Born in Missouri, Larry Dotson moved to Orange County, California at age 10. In the process of growing up in California, he won many awards for his illustrative skills. But it was the second prize in a Ford Motor Company illustration contest that fixed his career and opened the doors to a job in the aerospace industry. "Robert Wood impressed me most with his realistic seascapes. Also I took a variety of courses at Long Beach City College, I think only one was an art course. I didn't like school very much so winning the contest and getting the job with North American Rockwell came at just the right time." Larry worked with North American Rockwell and McDonell Douglas through the beginnings of the space shuttle designs. "When my job got too repetitious I wanted to be more creative so I opened my own studio and gallery. That was in 1972."

The Dotsons moved to Maui in 1983 where Larry could continue his love affair with the ocean. "Even while I was working for the aerospace industry, I was painting on my own, trying to capture the great power and calm embodied in the sea." Larry's subject matter has expanded just as Maui's colors have forced his palette to expand. "Ocean breezes through palms, sheer rock walls and tropical rainforests, incredible blue skies and golden sunsets...I doubt if I'll run out of material to paint."

Larry's style is also expanding as he tries new media and new ideas. Oil on canvas scenes painted in a photo-realistic fashion, which have become the hallmark of his work, are now accompanied by silk-screen and serigraph prints which display a more contemporary concern for the abstract elements of design. "I have no great ideal or romantic notion about my work," Larry says. "I have been successful with it and am getting better, and I'm able to feed my family with it. It's not work really, I enjoy painting too much to call it that."

Opposite page:
*Island Sunset
(Kahana), 16"x 20",
Oil, Private
Collection*

Na Pali Coast (Kauai), 11"x 14", Oil, Private Collection

MACARIO PASCUAL:

Monuments of the Moment

"A CLEAN DISSECTION THAT LAYS BARE THE HEART THAT IS ALL, THAT IS ENOUGH." MARCIA MORSE

Macario Pascual is a young painter, mature in his art, who presents moving images of local genre. Immigrating with his mother to Hawaii at age five, he joined his father, who was working for the sugar plantations. At age 13, he became the first and youngest recipient of the Lahaina Arts Society Art Scholarship. While he was still in high school the same society awarded Macario his first of many solo exhibitions. He studied art at the University of Hawaii, graduating with a BFA in Design, and returned immediately to Maui to pursue his painting full time.

Macario has cause to be proud of his accomplishments, having received commissions from the State of Hawaii and

The Laborer (Lahaina), 32"x 47½", Oil, Private Collection

Workers at Noon (Central Maui), 23½"x 32½", Oil, Private Collection

Alexander and Baldwin, Inc., and having been accepted in juried shows, winning awards locally and nationally. His *Hana Ko IV,* after receiving acceptance in the "Artists of Hawaii" exhibit of 1983, went on to Springfield, Massachusetts and the "National Exhibition of Contemporary Realism" where it received the "Muriel Ritchie Award" for oils. This painting is now in a private collection in New York. Another of his oils was selected for inclusion in the "Chautauque National Exhibition of American Art" in New York (one of 68 out of 2,600 entries). As of this writing, he holds invitations to two major group shows, one in San Francisco and the other in New Zealand.

In reviewing Pascual's work in a recent show, the *Star-Bulletin* art critic Marcia Morse wrote: "What seems to be significant in distinguishing the best genre painting...is a kind of leanness; ...the eye that cuts through [slice of life] must do so cleanly, so that no edges are torn, no blood let, only a clean dissection that lays bare the moment, the heart.... In the ongoing series of plantation images, *Workers at Noon* is clearly a masterwork. Suffused with an undertone of earth red—that color that permeates the air, the light, the skin— overlaid with a cool grey, the painting depicts three field workers whose implied sense of apprehension and off-center position suggest a larger and less certain fate."

Although Macario's interest in depicting Hawaii's plantation fields and laborers is still strong, he has been exploring other aspects of the milieu in which he lives and grew up as well as other techniques. In work such as *Young Boy in Rattan Chair* the scene shifts to an interior and glazes are introduced. In others we find him utilizing wax resist and ink. Pascual is certainly one of Maui's best "homegrown" talents and through his art speaks of people and places that are Maui in their essence.

The Caneworker (Puunene), 29½″ x 23½″, Oil, Private Collection

View from Tadashi Sato's Studio, 30" x 20", Oil, Private Collection

ROBERT LYN NELSON:

Seeking an Emotional Response

TIRED OF SHOWING WHALES BEING KILLED, I STARTED
TO PAINT THEM AS BEAUTIFUL CREATURES, SWIMMING FREE

R obert Lyn Nelson is perhaps the
first artist to really celebrate the
undersea world and he is certainly
one of America's foremost wildlife
and marine artists today. Robert
moved to Maui in 1977. "During the day I
enjoyed walking down to the small boat
harbor and sketching on the seawall. I'd sit
there for hours, wondering about the
whaleships that once anchored offshore. Who
were the men who sailed on these ships? Did
they think about their families back home?
What did they do in town? Were any of
them artists like me?"

As a child in Upland, California, Robert
learned perspective from his draftsman father,
who also taught him how to handle light and

shadow. He became proficient in watercolor
and charcoal. At fourteen he gained a full art
scholarship to Mount San Antonio College in
Pomona and at eighteen took his first
vacation: to Hawaii. "The compositions of
Pieter De Hooch are practically infallible. I've
also been influenced by Rembrandt,
especially in his use of multiple light sources,
and Constable. He would sometimes spend
six years on a painting to perfect it. I admire
that kind of discipline. I am very much
interested in the honesty of these proven
old masters."

Turning down an appointment to San
Francisco's Academy of Arts, Robert moved
into a rented beach house in Laie with some
friends. "While living at Laie, I started to

Reflections of Lahaina, Acrylic on Canvas, Tryptich, Three 48″ x 36″ panels, Private Collection

study local culture. I went to the library and borrowed lots of books about Hawaii and the Pacific. Polynesian legends held my fascination for awhile and I did numerous drawings and paintings of the ancient gods, warriors and folk heroes."

After moving to Maui, the history of Lahaina became a fascination for the young artist, and the old capitol's whaling era dominated much of his painting. "I did a lot of illustrative-type work and made a good living selling them through the galleries. My studio was full of ships, spouting whales, and men with harpoons.

"Finally I just got tired of showing whales being killed. I started to paint them as beautiful creatures, swimming free and peaceful in their underwater environment. Although my future art will certainly touch many new subjects, these whales will remain for me a never-ending source of inspiration."

The first of Robert's "underwater-abovewater" scenes was painted in 1979 and led to immediate success and subsequent widespread recognition of his entire range of work. "My aim is to cause a reaction in viewers when they look at my work. I want them to have an emotional response that comes close to the way I feel when actually painting.

The above is based on material written by Ronn Ronck, *Honolulu Advertiser,* and Robert Taylor.

Opposite page: *Impressions of Hong Kong City Lights,*
24"x 36", Acrylic and Oils
Right: *Baby Harp Seal, 40"x 30", Arylic*
Below: *Hanalei Pasture, 30"x 40", Acrylic and Oils*

CECELIA RODRIGUEZ:

Under the Spreading Banyan

A MASTER OF BLACK VELVET, THIS LAHAINA LADY
IS STILL EXPLORING NEW TECHNIQUES, NEW HORIZONS

The crowd you spotted under the banyan tree in Lahaina was very likely watching Cecelia Rodriguez painting acrylic scenery or bird studies on hand-colored rice paper. At age 65, she can still put in 12 hours a day painting, teaching or giving demonstrations. "I don't do the velvets any more, it's mostly oils on canvas and collages."

Cecelia, whose father was an art director in motion pictures for 30 years, was born in California. "I still see his name, William Schmit, in the credits. He worked for Universal and then Fox. I guess I picked up some talent from him." Cecelia grew up in the Culver City area, married, and eventually moved to Reno, Nevada, where she worked in an electronics firm which was a sub-contractor for a large aircraft corporation.

After a vacation visit to Hawaii in 1960, Cecelia moved out, taking up hotel and restaurant studies at Kapiolani Community College. "I started painting in 1965 while living in Waikiki and moved to Lahaina in 1969. I painted on black velvet until 1970."

That year, 1970 was a turning point year for Cecelia. The Lahaina Arts Society refused to accept velvet paintings as a legitimate medium. "It's a difficult medium to work, you must work slowly with thin paint. You really just stain or dye the velvet under strong lights over a period of six weeks. Anyway, the Society's decision not to accept my work forced me to grow. I decided to take a trip to Australia where I learned to work with oils on canvas." Cecelia, already famous for her black velvets, toured Australia giving demonstrations in one medium while learning a whole range of new techniques. She returned to give her most successful one-woman show "Faces of the Pacific" at the Lahaina Arts Society.

Since then she has branched into collage work, her current focus. In this medium Cecelia uses hand-colored rice papers or papers she prepares with acrylics. And her themes have shifted from oil portraiture to paper floral arrangements. "Maui is a good place for artists. Even the not-so-good artists have a chance to be seen...I don't have any special message with my art, I work for my own satisfaction and the pleasure people get from my work."

Cecelia gives classes to children and the aged, exhibits and demonstrations at the Maui Surf Hotel, and she can still be found on Saturdays under the banyan tree.

Opposite page:
Iris, 16"x 20", Oil on hand colored rice paper
Right: *Paniolo, 20"x 24", Oil on canvas*

STEPHEN SANDS:

A South Sea Crucible

TO CREATE A CHRONICLE OF THE BEAUTY, DELICACY AND ROMANCE THAT IS HAWAII

The palette knife is definitely my favorite tool," says Stephen Sands. "It would take ages to achieve the same effect with a brush. And some things can only be done with a knife.... I generally use a brush for the background and the palette knife for the foreground to gain depth and contrast."

Stephen came to Hawaii from Rhode Island for relaxation in 1964. He was so successful at the Honolulu Zoo Fence and Sunday Art Marts, selling his whimsical animals on black velvet and island scenes on canvas, that he was able to move to Maui a year later. And while Stephen hadn't come to Hawaii planning to paint, he had the right background—four years of art and architecture at the Rhode Island School of

Design including scenic painting with the late Gordon Harris.

Once on Maui, Stephen continued to perfect his technique by studing with Joyce Clark—"a superb impressionist and wizard with a palette knife"—and the noted Bennett Bradbury. Dissatisfied with painting only part of the time, Stephen left Maui in 1972 to explore the South Pacific. "I lived on a shoestring, selling my paintings as I went— sometimes before the paint was dry."

He created more than seventy-five paintings in the seven-and-a-half-month odyssey. Painting and giving demonstrations, Stephen traveled from Tahiti to Moorea, south to New Zealand and on to New Caledonia, the New Hebrides, Fiji, Tonga and Samoa. He returned to Maui with renewed

First Snow Haleakala, 24"x 36", Oil

vigor and confidence to begin what has become a very productive career, recording with oils on canvas the "beauty, delicacy and romance that is Hawaii.

"My studios on Maui and at Princeville on Kauai are perfect for artists. I love the mountains, sea and sunshine." He also enjoys people and teaching, averaging fifty students a week in five or six separate classes. For the last ten years, he has also held four "classroom style" night classes and two "out on location" classes each week for the Hawaii State Board of Education. Stephen also travels to the leper colony at Kalaupapa to give demonstrations and lessons.

In both his work and his teaching, Stephen's purpose has been to provide for people who love Hawaii, the same kind of beauty that he gave to the peoples of the South Pacific when he painted their major islands. To achieve this kind of visual chronicle, Stephen does most of his work on location and encourages his students to do the same. And "painting is not always as peaceful as it looks. Often the picture that appears effortless was a battlefield in the making."

To provide greater access to his work, Stephen has created several series of serigraph prints. These and his paintings are available at the Sands Studio and Gallery, which he started and still operates in the Lahaina Shores Village.

SANDS, *Makamakaole Gulch Waterfall,* 36"x 48", Oil

ANDREA SMITH:

Artist with a Torch

UNIVERSAL MESSAGES ABOUT BALANCING THE EARTH AND OURSELVES; ABOUT HUMANITY BLENDING IN HARMONY

*T*he message is always the same although the images change. "When I was in second grade, I won an art contest with a painting of two skunks facing each other, a boy skunk holding a bottle of perfume and a girl skunk holding a flower. It's really the same theme today."

Andrea Smith was born and raised in Detroit, Michigan. She pursued a teaching career, receiving a B.A. in Education from Wayne State University, and spent ten years in the classroom. These teaching years broadened Andrea's perception of people and reinforced the notion that underneath all the diversity we are one people on one planet.

Not long before leaving teaching to paint full time one of Andrea's students asked her, "Why do you care when I don't?" And Andrea, who couldn't really answer this question, shifted her energies to an area where her caring would hopefully meet with understanding, or at least less resistance.

In January of 1981, Andrea moved to Maui with her husband and their two children. "The move has been an absolute blessing. I feel much closer to nature." And while nature provides inspiration for Andrea her paintings are idea- or message-centered, "...physical representations of what I believe metaphysically.

"The patterns in my work represent energy

Above: *Budda Consciousness 1984, 22"x 30", Watercolor, Private Collection*
Opposite page: *Uniting to Raise Earths Consciousness, 22"x 30", Watercolor*
Below: *Putting Out the Message of Love, 22"x 30", Watercolor*

to me. The invisible forces, movements and relationships are what I look for. The paintings are not pre-planned, they flow through me. My greatest desire is to help others find peace within themselves...lower self, middle self and higher self...The act of integrating these selves is what I paint about. The message I want to get across is peace."

Gaugain, Picasso, Miro, Chagall are all painters Andrea admires. She sees her paintings as "Abstract realism," and uses standard sizes as the most comfortable for what she is trying to do. Andrea has worked in a variety of different media, watercolors, ink and pastels mostly, but finds watercolors the most enjoyable.

This young artist sports a long list of juried exhibitions and one-woman and group shows which began for her in Detroit at the Gallery Renaissance. Her watercolors can be seen in the Lahaina and Kapalua galleries, the Houshang Gallery, Texas, Midtown Gallery, Washington, D.C., and the Volcano Art Center on the Big Island.

MAPES, *Pineapple Corner, 18"x 36", Oil, Private Collection*

LOWELL MAPES:

Light, Color and Feeling

PAINTING IS REALLY A NON-INTELLECTUAL ACTIVITY
THE MESSAGE, IF THERE IS ONE, IS NON-VERBAL

As a young man born and raised in Los Angeles, California, Lowell Mapes moved to Lahaina in 1972. "I sort of backed into the painting. I did a few pen and ink drawings which sold right away, and that started it." Lowell has worked over the years at a variety of jobs such as washing windows and driving a truck. He was influenced greatly by Peter Hayward: "He and I were friends for quite awhile and Peter encouraged me a lot. I gained a deeper perception of nature from him—learning to look outward, rather than inward." With the help of friends and patrons, Lowell has perfected his craft and emerged in 1974 and '75 as a major talent.

A rewarding trip to Europe reinforced his studies of the great masters. Lowell was influenced by "those painters more concerned with freshness of vision than with

Yellow Boat, 18"x 24", Oil, Private Collection

Chicken Coop,
20" x 24", Oil

style—the Baroque painters, especially Frans Hals. Artists like Rembrandt and Rubens, for all their skill as draftsmen, were all too often hindered by convention and technique. The romantics, always idealizing, were the same. On the positive side, I like seeing the way Monet, Corot or Velasquez perceive their world...Gauguin for what he does with the flat shape of his painting."

Talking with Lowell one cannot help but appreciate how well-read he is. He very easily shared observations on art and artists by Hemingway, Sylvester and numerous other writers. When asked about the reading, he said he was giving it up; that reading was a distraction. Lowell's major concerns are the "perceptions and tensions" in paintings. He worked with watercolor for quite some time before going into the oils for which he has become most noted. "I like the oils because I can go back into a painting, creating more depth or make small adjustments." He sees himself as still growing and learning, and plans another trip to Europe shortly.

I don't think being on Maui has made any real difference in my art," Lowell said. "This is not really an isolated place." He refers of course to his style and method of working, for his subjects or images are drawn from the local surroundings. "I really love to work outside, on location. A good ninety percent of my work is done outside. I feel a lot closer to nature and get a better sense of colors and energies about the subject."

Lowell has been exhibited in numerous shows here and on the mainland and acquired some distinctive awards in the process. His recent paintings may be seen at the Village Gallery in Lahaina.

INDEX OF ARTISTS

"**ARTISTS OF MAUI**" ORDER FORM

PLEASE PRINT CLEARLY:

Mail to me: Name _____

Address _____

City _____ State _____ Zip _____

Mail as a gift to: Name _____

Address _____

City _____ State _____ Zip _____

☐ Gift card from: _____

Mail as a gift to: Name _____

Address _____

City _____ State _____ Zip _____

☐ Gift card from: _____

Mail as a gift to: Name _____

Address _____

City _____ State _____ Zip _____

☐ Gift card from: _____

QUANTITY	PRICE	SUB–TOTAL
	$24.95 per book	
Hawaii State residents add 4% sales tax		
Shipping and Handling add $3.00 per book		
TOTAL ENCLOSED		

Make checks payable to: SUMAC Publishing
P.O. Box 1646 • Makawao, HI 96768 • Ph. (808) 572–9565